Illuminating the Mundane

Illuminating the Mundane

Transformative Silk Painting and Haiku

Billie Ruth Furuichi

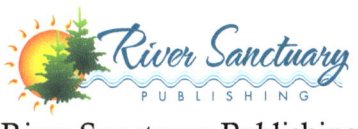

River Sanctuary Publishing
Felton, California

Illuminating the Mundane: Transformative Silk Painting and Haiku

Copyright © 2010 by Billie Ruth Furuichi

All artwork and haiku are copyrighted creations of Billie Ruth Furuichi
email: bilichki@gmail.com

Cover and interior design by River Sanctuary Graphic Arts
ISBN 978-0-9841140-5-4

Printed in the United State of America

Additional copies available from:
www.riversanctuarypublishing.com
and
Amazon.com

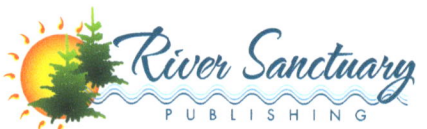

River Sanctuary Publishing
P.O. Box 1561
Felton, CA 95018
www.riversanctuarypublishing.com
Dedicated to the awakening of the New Earth

ACKNOWLEDGMENTS

Over the years, I have written many workbooks to accompany workshops. But I have always dreamed of publishing a full color presentation of my silk paintings and digital collages. Were it not for Annie Elizabeth Porter, my publisher at River Sanctuary Publishing, who first suggested this type of art book with haiku side-by-side, I may never have realized this dream. Annie Elizabeth had the perfect idea, but when she asked me to write the preface and introduction, I found myself including my whole life story. Thanks to the watchful eye of my astute but gentle editor, David Weiss, I was able to understand which text was necessary, and which could be saved for another book. I extend my profound thanks to David and Annie, for having the patience to work with me over the past year and guide my fingertips over the keys. Their work at River Sanctuary Publishing is fulfilling and creative. I see them having financial abundance and soul-filled success in all of their upcoming exciting projects. I also extend a big hug and thank you to my husband, Isamu, who has finally figured out that when I'm at the computer every weekend, he's probably going to be fixing his own lunch. When Isamu sees the haiku he wrote at age 12, along with his photographic images embedded into some of my digital collages, I am confident he will know that making all those Top Ramen bowls was well worth it. And, of course, last and most importantly, I would never have become who I truly am without the wise and talented Aunt Ruth Puchek, who not only taught me to paint on silk, but showed me at a very early age how to find and release my own creativity. Aunt Ruth always said, "Trust yourself, Billie Ruth, and know to STOP painting when the painting is finished!"

CONTENTS

INTRODUCTION

The images and haiku in this collection represent my own spiritual journey since 1986, which has involved a process of consciously feeding my soul through artistic expression, whether it be dancing, writing poetry, haiku, or painting silk. Living in this mundane day-to-day world, I will shrivel up and die if I shut out the ethereal voices of creativity pleading with me to wake up, honor the needs of my soul, and get back to the process of creating something! When I do not listen – when I forget who I truly am as a spiritual being – when I go to work day after day with my feet getting more and more stuck in the stuff of this world, I suffer from it, whether it's a cold or a bad back. Yes, it is all too easy to be seduced by mundane daily realities, thinking that we can solve other people's problems, or watching reality TV to feel comparatively better about our own lives, but seduction means we are asleep – not keeping our eye on the bright light of our own creative soul. Painting silks and writing haiku are among the ways I have kept my light bright. In the process, I can also help to illuminate bits of this mundane world, making it meaningful for me, and I hope for those of you reading this book.

Each image is accompanied by original haiku, capturing the intention as a healing icon. Haiku is a form of Japanese poetry, consisting of three lines which make a metaphorical statement. The first line is an observation or statement about nature, philosophy or spirit in five syllables. The second line unfolds as an implication or an alternative layer of reality, in seven syllables. The third line reveals an epiphany or irony connecting the previous two at a higher level, in five syllables. This structure is mirrored in my haiku creations. My art is abstract and impressionistic in the same way that haiku is a condensed metaphoric expression that carries strong connections to nature and spirit suggesting a visual image. In that way, I think haiku works well symbolically with my artistic style. Traditionally, haiku concerns itself with human emotions rather than human acts, which is also true of my artwork. I think of artistic expression as a bridge and my job is to build that bridge so that the observer can cross it successfully over into my way of perceiving the world. Sometimes it takes both words and images to bring you into my vision. For that reason, I like to include haiku into each art piece. I also use symbols from Japanese Kanji, Greek and Hebrew, as another way of showing how each piece speaks to me. These words and phrases add universality to the meaning – what truths might be embedded there, and why I was guided to paint it.

The first image, *Yellow Hibiscus*, was my very first silk painting, followed by, *Fragrant Meditations*, which is one of the most recent digital collages, combining two silk paintings and a photograph of Fuchsias. This juxtaposition demonstrates not only a shift in style and focus, but also my growth as an artist. Seven images that follow are from The Transformation Wheel™, a collection of 3' x 6' banners hanging in a circle, like a huge windsock, that I use during my workshops.

The next eight images (10 through 18) are early attempts at digital collage, accomplishing what I had envisioned for years – translucent, intermingled, overlapped layers. I just can't do that sort of thing with cut and paste collage since actual pieces of fabric didn't show through one another well enough to accomplish what I had in my mind's eye. But with digital collage, it all came together. These pieces are the result of playing with new and wonderful technology.

Images 19 through 23 are close-ups of three separate original silk paintings, without enhancement layers. Images 24 through 33 represent the next phase of working with digital collage, incorporating photography by my husband, Isamu, as well as multiple layers. Image number 34, *Wise Fish*, is a close up of silk paints on bamboo cotton, which I made into a Kaftan blouse. Number 35, *Gravity, Escaping*, is strictly an afternoon's doodle on Valentine's Day this year, using crayons and markers. When I was finished, I realized it expressed my theory about gravity, so using a gold pen, I wrote around the edges using the words I had received in meditation. The final two images are actual silk collages made from pieces of a large work I had used for wallpaper, then tried removing it when we sold our house. They are both enhanced with Japanese Kanji, Greek and Hebrew letterings representing the haiku that appear on the pages beside them.

If you have been attracted to this book, you are most likely an artist or have a soul of the artist within you. It is my belief that we are all artists, and there is some creative creature inside yearning to break loose and express itself. Listen to it! Even natural artists like myself, who have grown up with the freedom to create and support for their creative side, need to prepare for a consciousness shift – where soul can meet Spirit. By that, I mean, preparation to illuminate the mundane through movement and breath. Just because we live in a mundane daily world, doesn't mean we have to get stuck in it. Silk painting has proven for me, to be a powerful way to awaken me at the deepest level, open my heart chakra, invite Spirit to move into my soul, and express what is inside of me – the Kingdom of Heaven. It's also a fun way just to release, relax, and simply play. My hope is that you will begin to feel this shift into your own ethereal being, as you thumb through this book and are perhaps inspired to spend some quality time with yourself, writing haiku, painting silk, learning digital collage.

Illuminating the Mundane

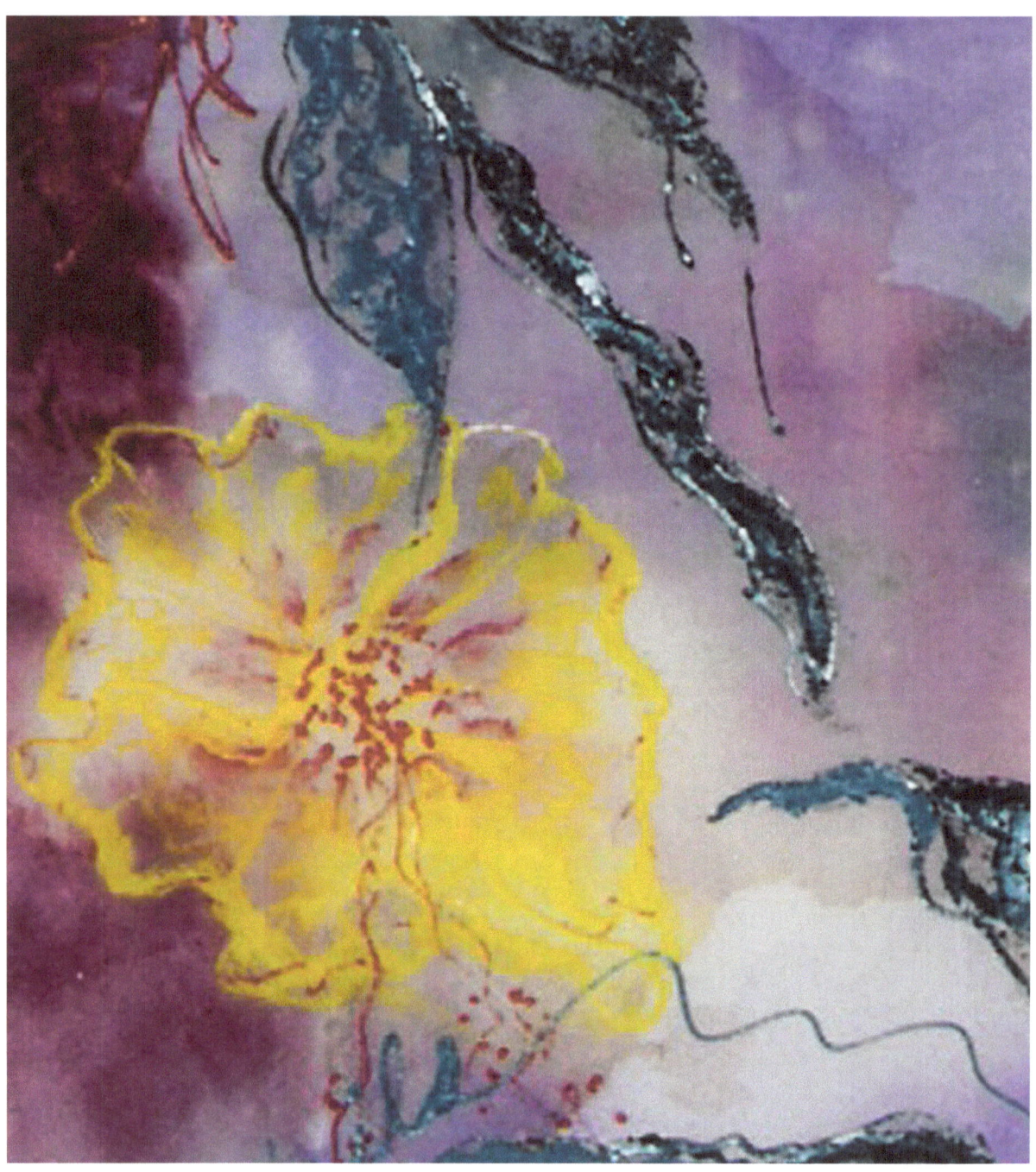

© Billie Ruth Furuichi

Plate No.1 — Yellow Hibiscus

Yellow Hybiscus

Transparent petals will dry

to make healing tea

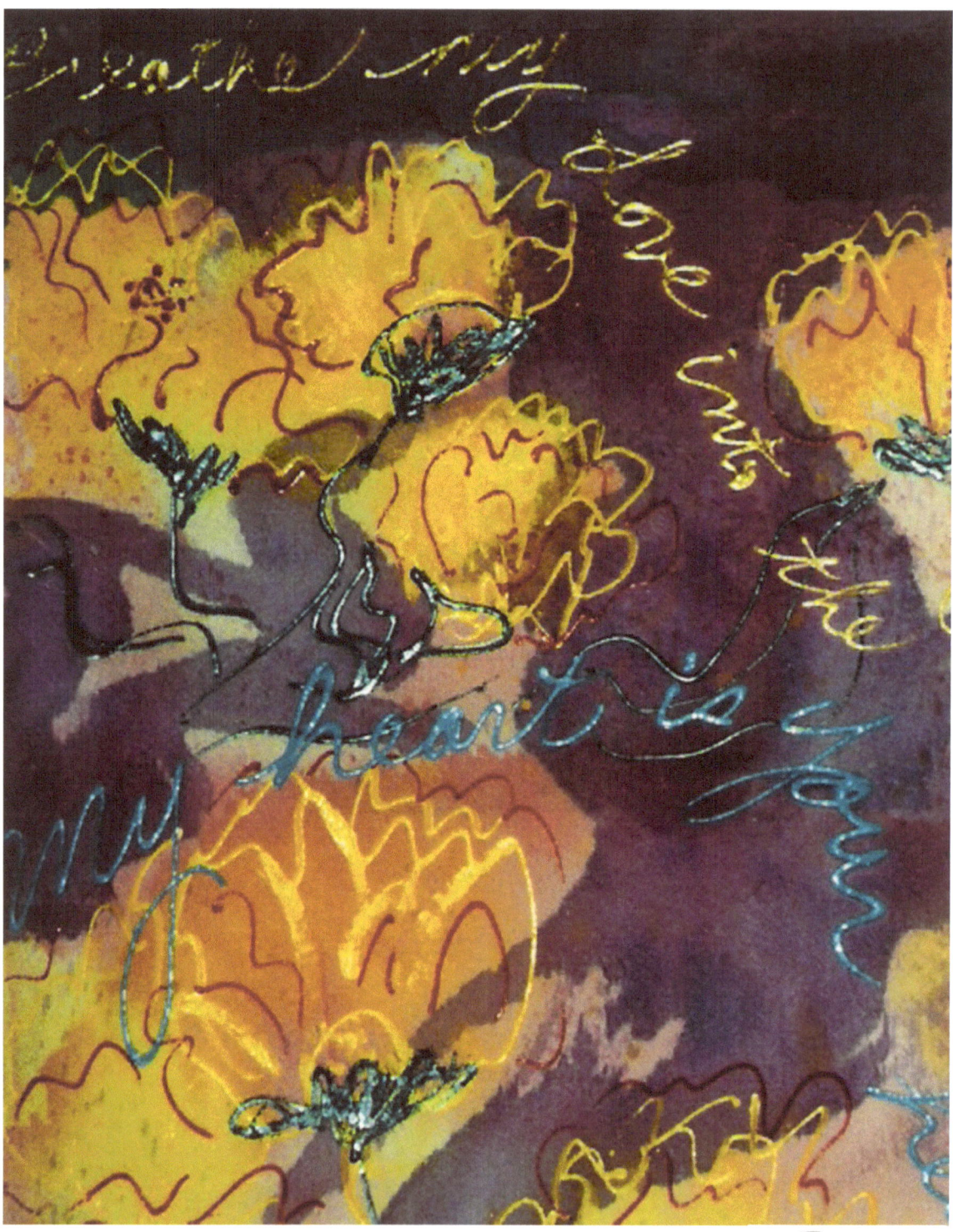

Plate No.2 — Fragrant Meditations

Breathe love to corners

Fragrant meditations rise

Love shall overcome

☯

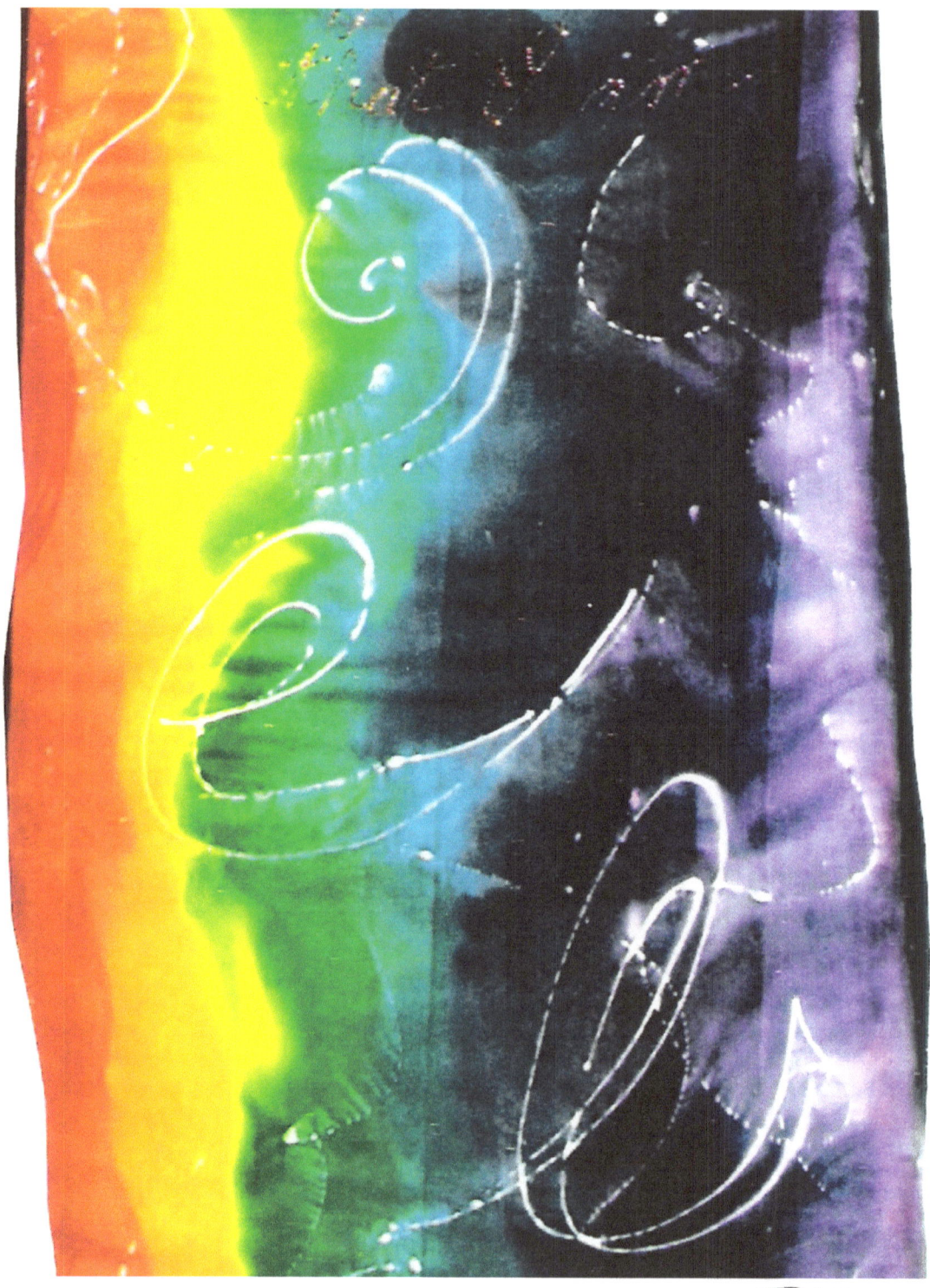

Plate No.3 — Release

© Billie Ruth Furuichi

Release to the one

center I Am that I Am

Balancing the earth

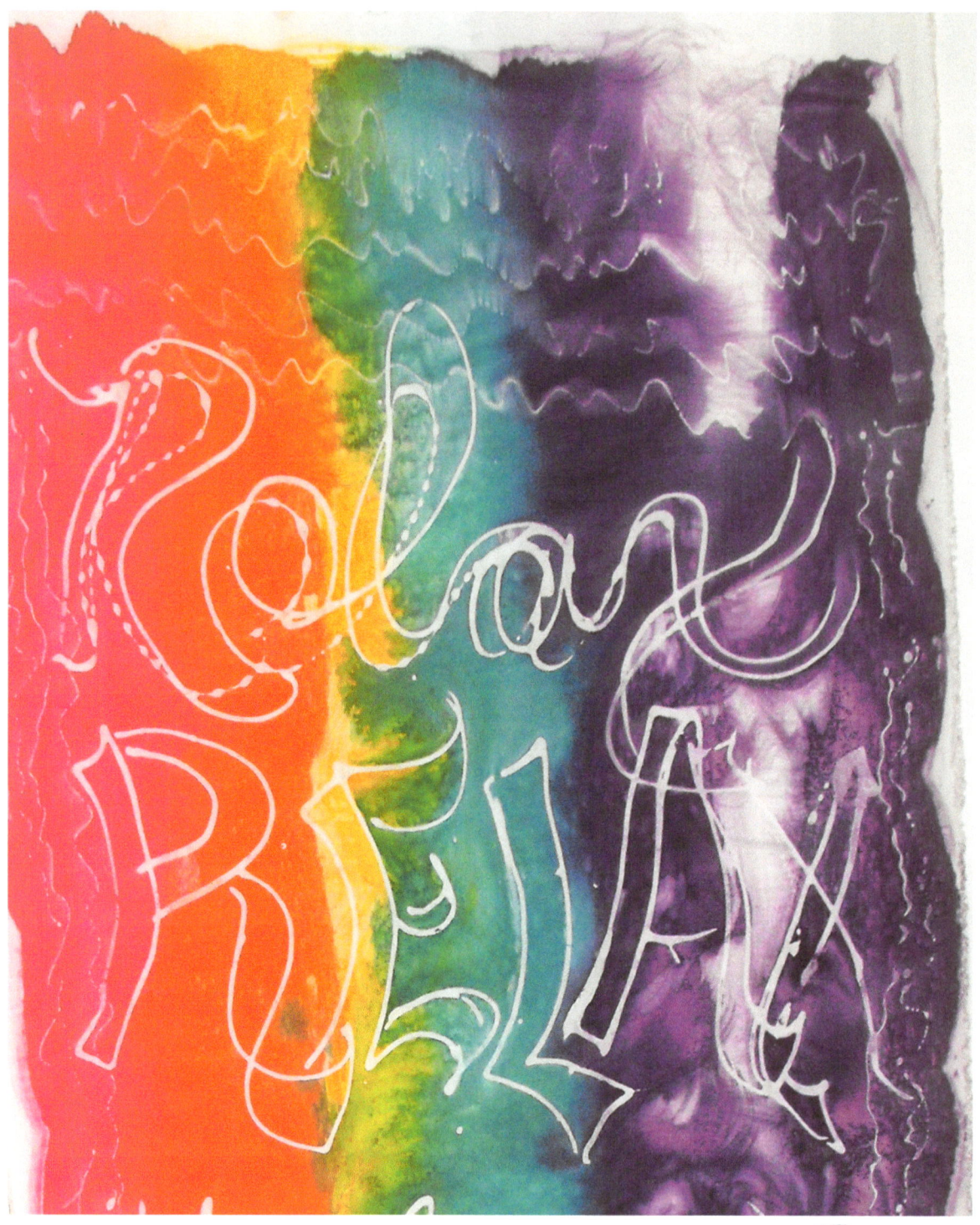

Plate No.4 — Relax

© Billie Ruth Furuichi

Relax and Be Still

deep within my soul I sigh

Healing is at hand

☯

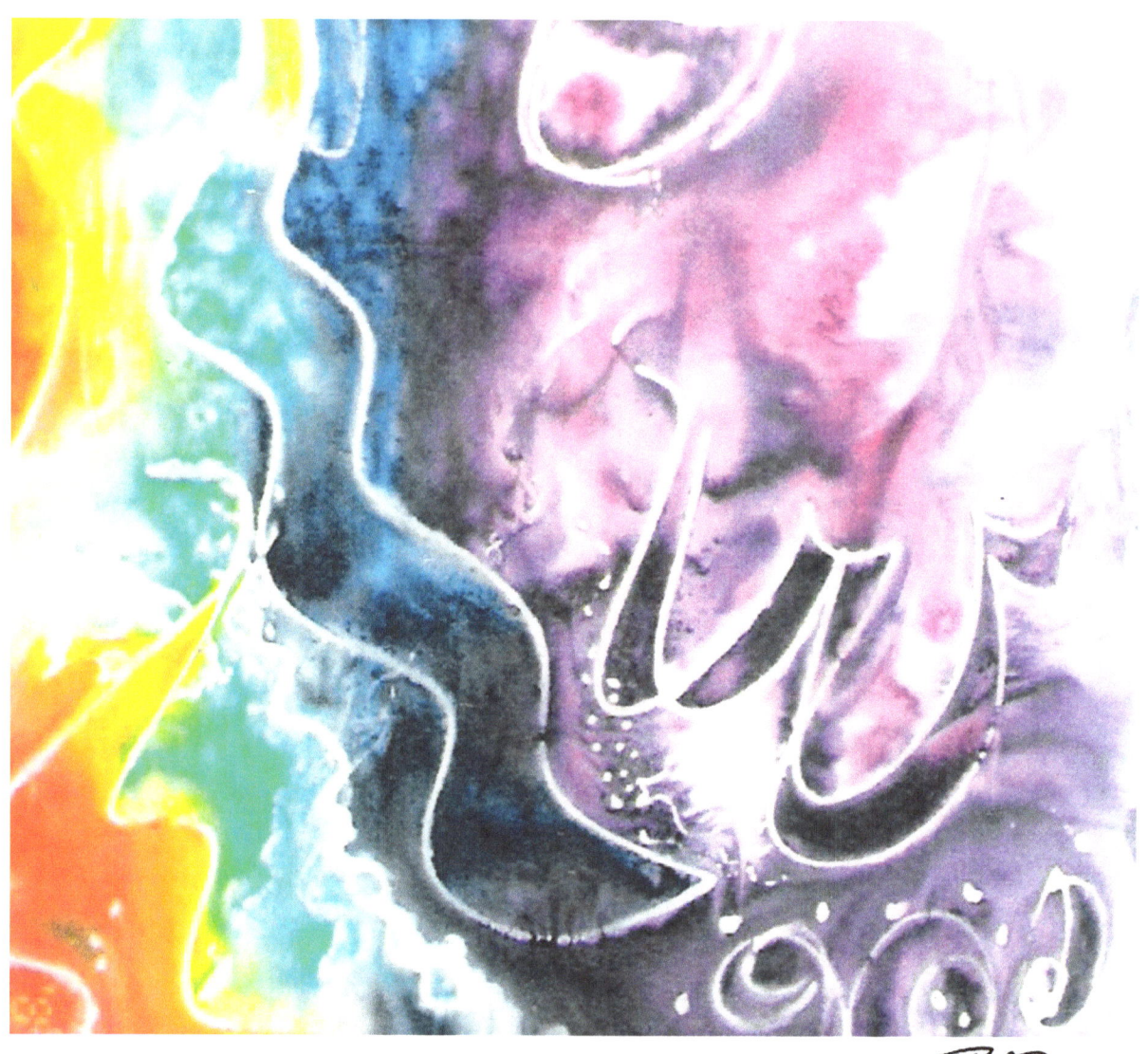

© Billie Ruth Furuichi

Plate No.5 — Flow

Release, Relax, Flow

Regeneration begins

from the inside, out

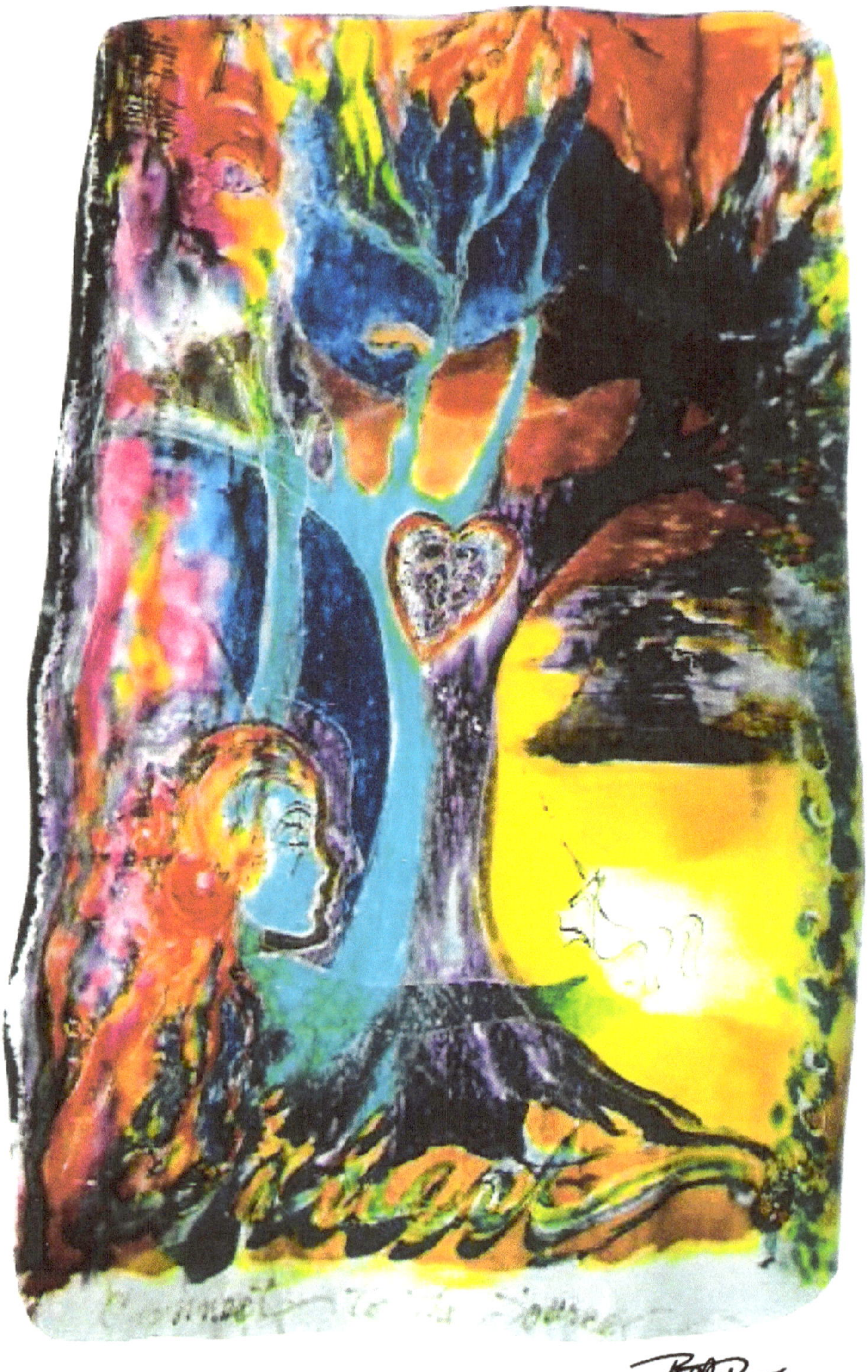

Plate No.6 — Connect

Unicorn alone

Standing in his dreams
of light

Teaching us to sing

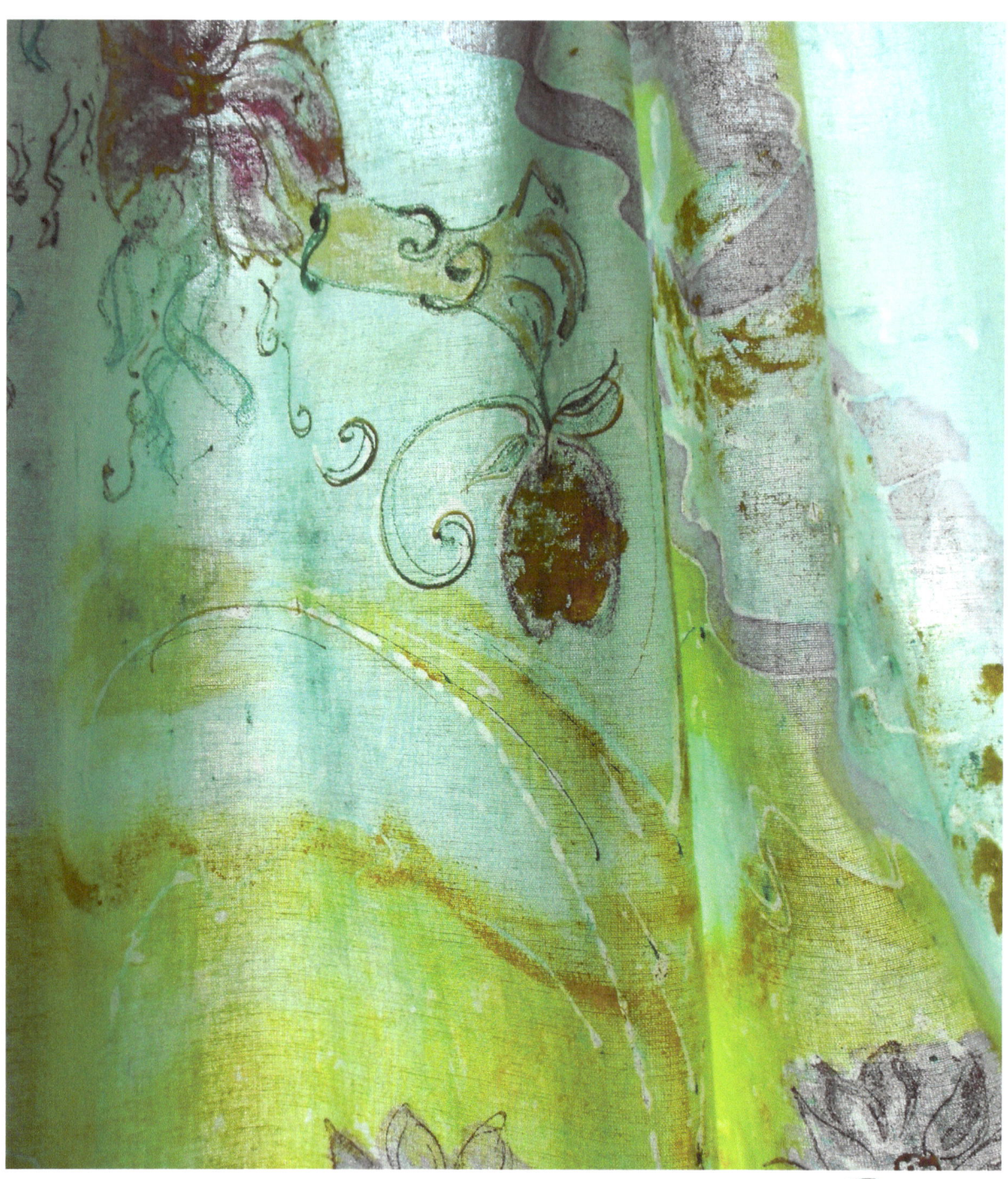

© Billie Ruth Furuichi

Plate No.7 — Offer the Apple

Offer the apple

Step back lovingly
detached

Await its return

☯

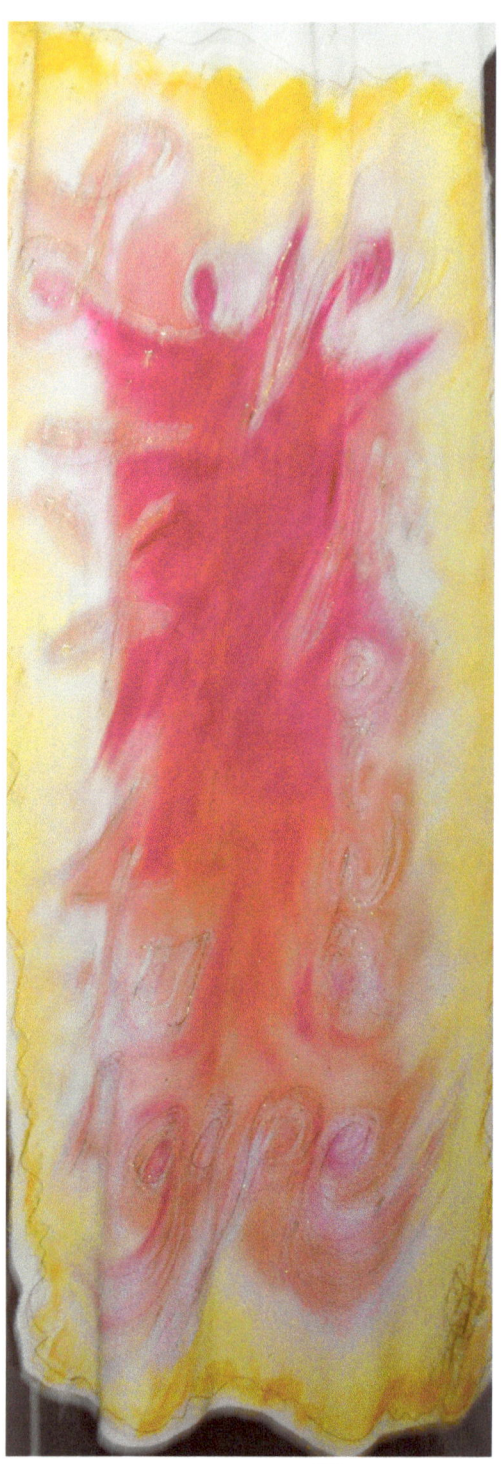

Plate No.8 — Love

© Billie Ruth Furuichi

We are Agape

Dissolving all veils of fear

Love shall overcome

☯

COMMENTARY ONE

ON DOING WHAT COMES NATURALLY

In 1986, I developed a workshop in leadership and decision-making for youth exchanges between Maui and Russia, using a big poster I called the *Transformation Wheel*™, which outlined essential steps for the kids to write their own action plans during youth summit meetings. After four years, I took a job teaching English in Japan, where I met and married Isamu Furuichi, a Master Chef with an impressive Samurai Warrior-Monk lineage from the early 1500's. We moved back to my hometown in Denver, Colorado, where a natural integration of movement meditation, haiku and silk painting evolved. This "integration" came about because Aunt Ruth had taught me how to paint silk a few years before I married Isamu. Aunt Ruth also wrote haiku for her original water color art cards and scarves that sold throughout the Hawaiian Islands.

Isamu would tell me about his ancestor's castle in the Yamoto Province, and stories about gatherings where hundreds of guests would lounge in hot springs drinking tea and sake, while listening to the head of the Furuichi household, a Samauri Warrior Monk, named Harima, recite his latest haiku. Isamu's haiku found its way into a silk scarf of dark blue trees and empty footprints across a field of snow:

> *Yuki no yoru – Ashiato hitotsu – Kaerimichi*
>
> *Snow falling at night – Follow black footprints alone – Finding my way home*

In our basement studio, I would put on meditation music, stretch the silk, draw a flowing design and write a haiku with the acrylic resist. The process of silk painting starts with drawing a design in the acrylic resist, which means you have to paint blind since the resist is clear when it goes onto the white, transparent silk. I realized that my workshops, which were becoming more spiritual in focus, needed a silk banner for each word in the Transformation Wheel™. Painting them was movement meditation in itself, as I moved the paints directly onto the silk fibers quickly, letting the vibrant silk paints flow into each other, sweeping them down the length of the banner. Seven banners became the new Transformation Wheel® for these workshops.

The first three banners carry the words **Release**, **Relax** and **Flow**, in a bright array of rainbow colors. The fourth word, **Connect**, became a representational landscape between the earthly and the cosmos. The fifth word, **Love**, became three dancers weaving through bright pink colors. I painted the banner for **Let-Go** after my mother had made her transition. It is done in vibrant greens with many hands reaching up toward the words, as if in the process of letting go of the words themselves. The final banner, **Regenerate**, is a stylistic Madonna in pink, ultra-violet and gold.

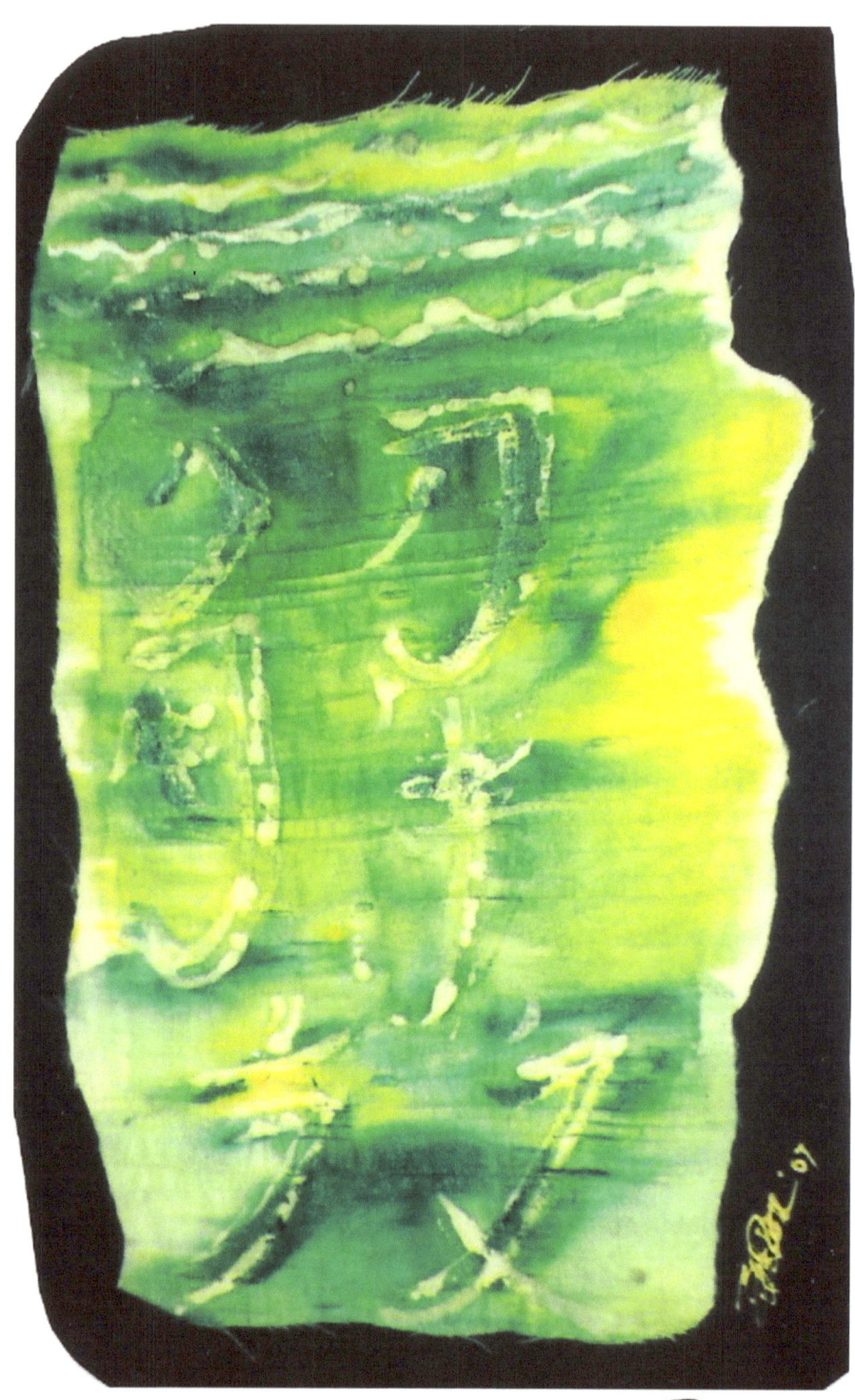

Plate No.9 — Kaiho Iki

© Billie Ruth Furuichi

Kaiho Iki Chi

Illuminating darkness

Oh, my path is clear!

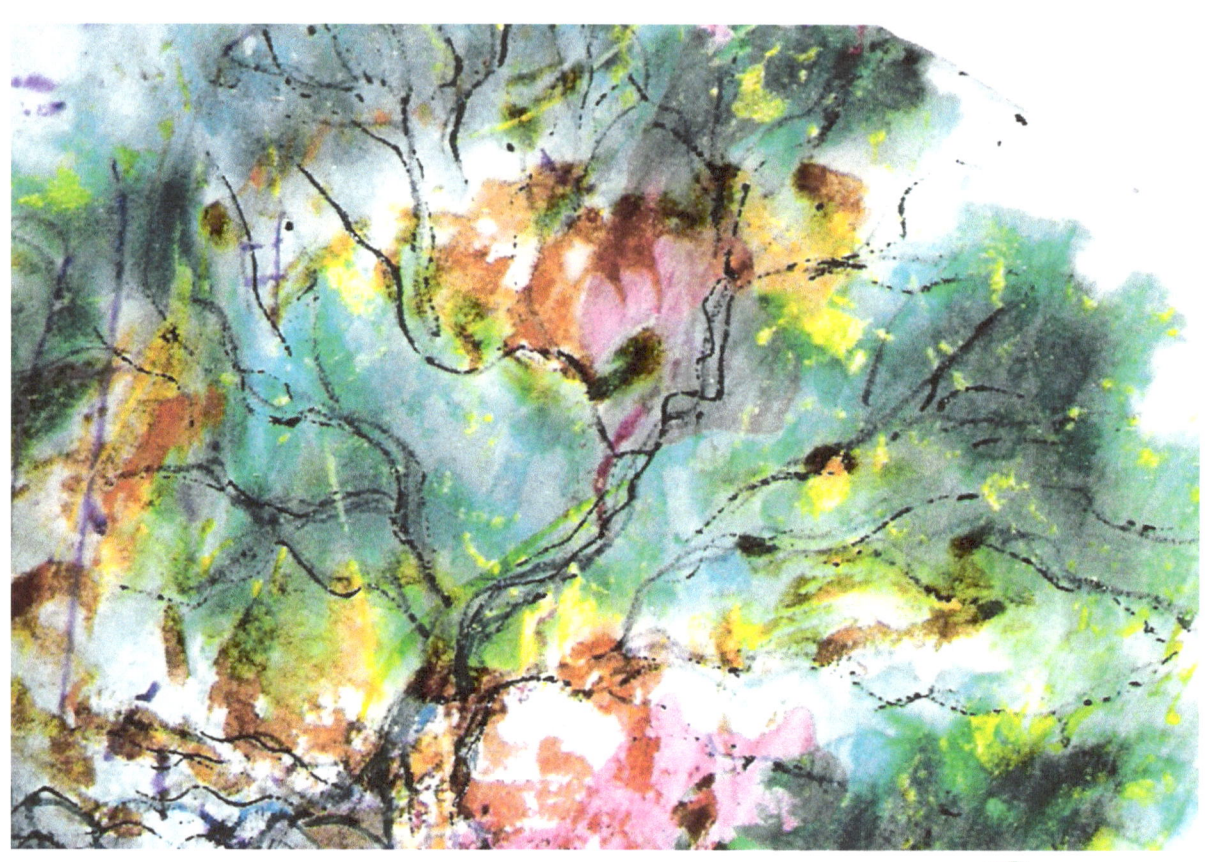

© Billie Ruth Furuichi

Plate No.10 — Tree of Life 1

Lead me to a Tree

Delicious bite of crisp Truth

Giving me knowledge

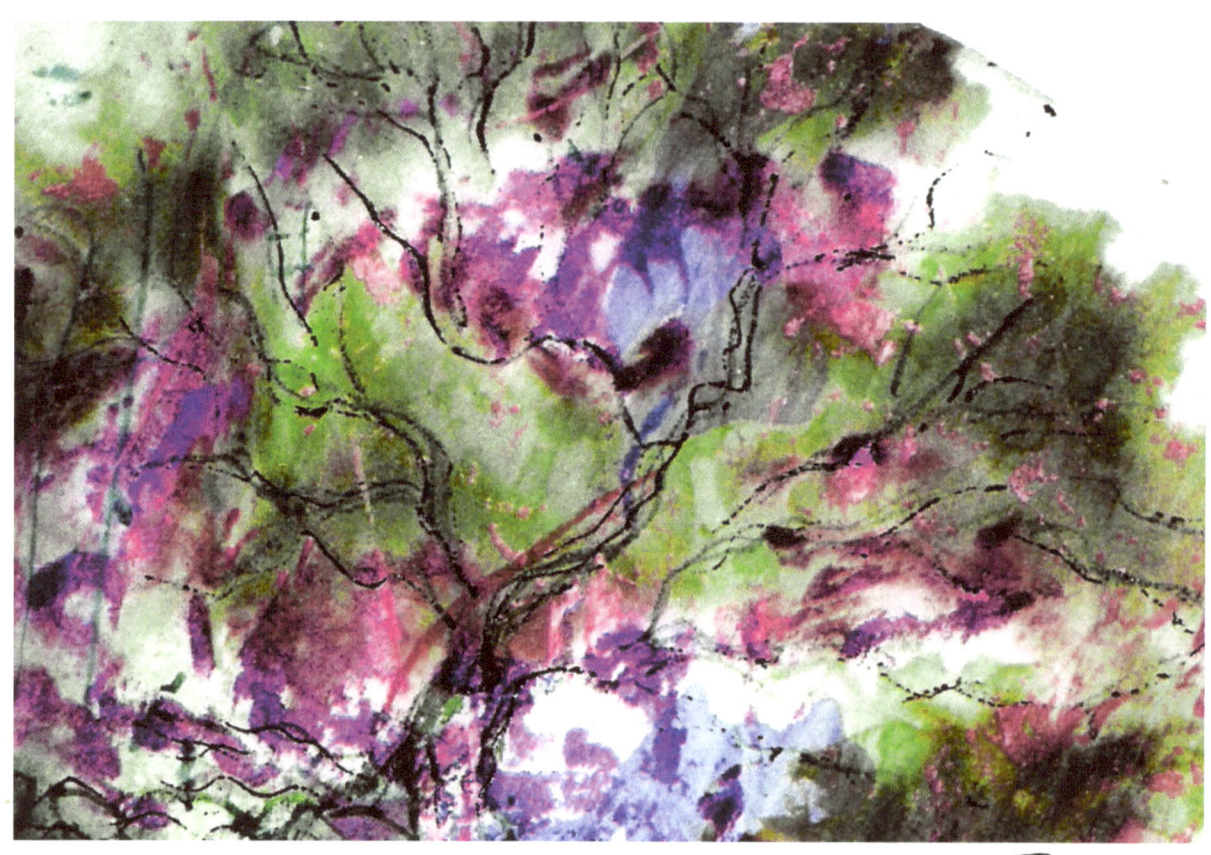

© Billie Ruth Furuichi

Plate No.11 — Tree of Life 2

Chill of Fall on leaves

Never expecting to stay

Envisioning Spring

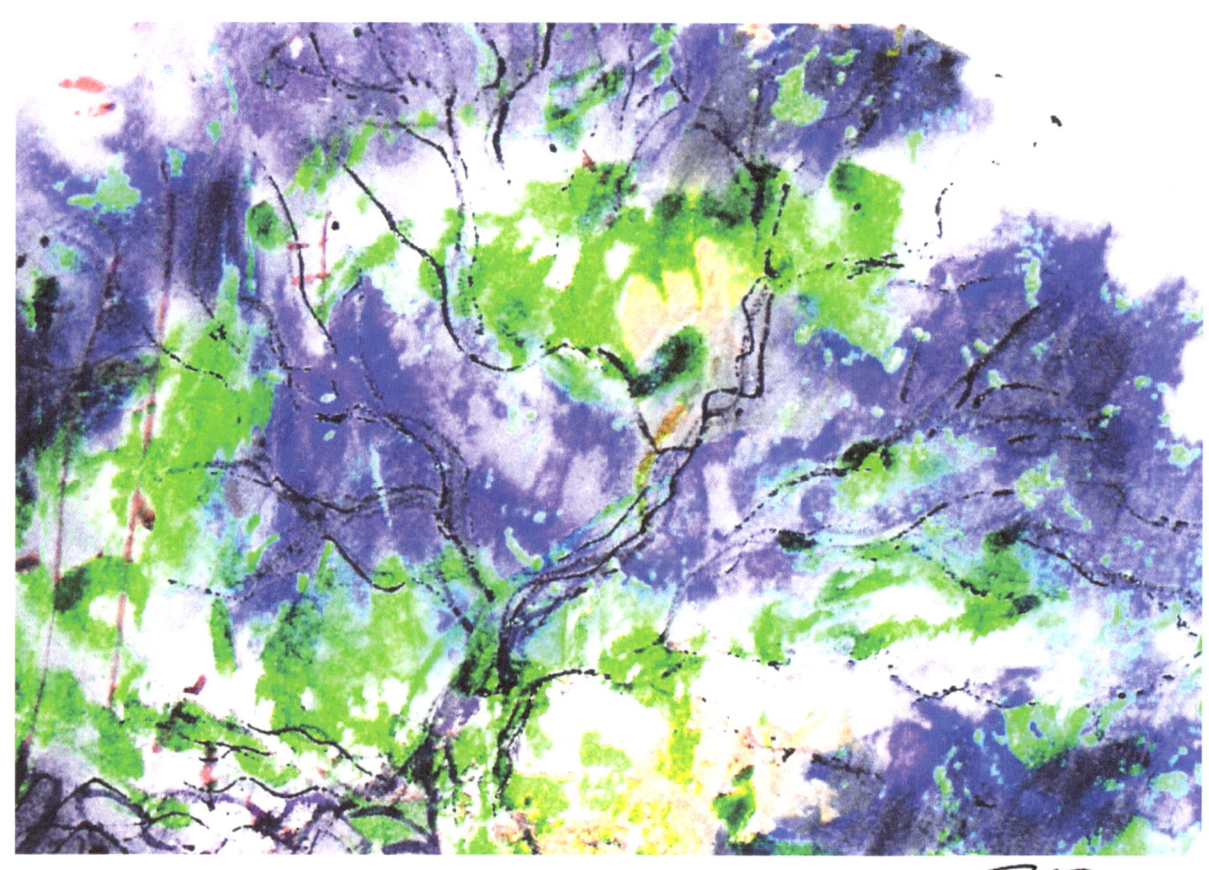

© Billie Ruth Furuichi

Plate No.12 — Tree of Life 3

Lion in Winter

Sleeping with the lamb
in peace

Dreaming the same dream

☯

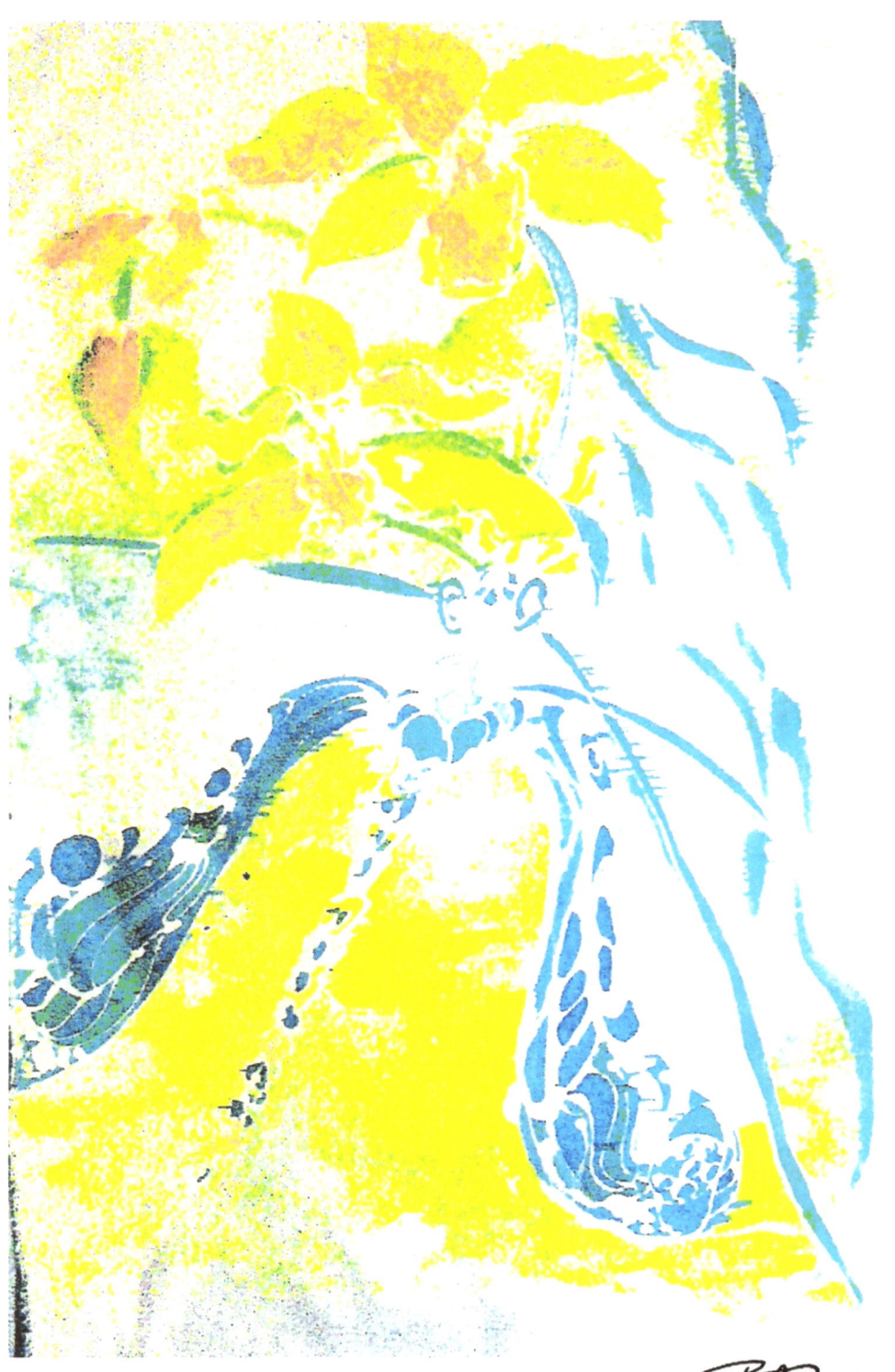

Plate No.13 — Dragonfly Diva

© Billie Ruth Furuichi

Dragonfly disspells

History of hardened shell

Oh, she flies so free!

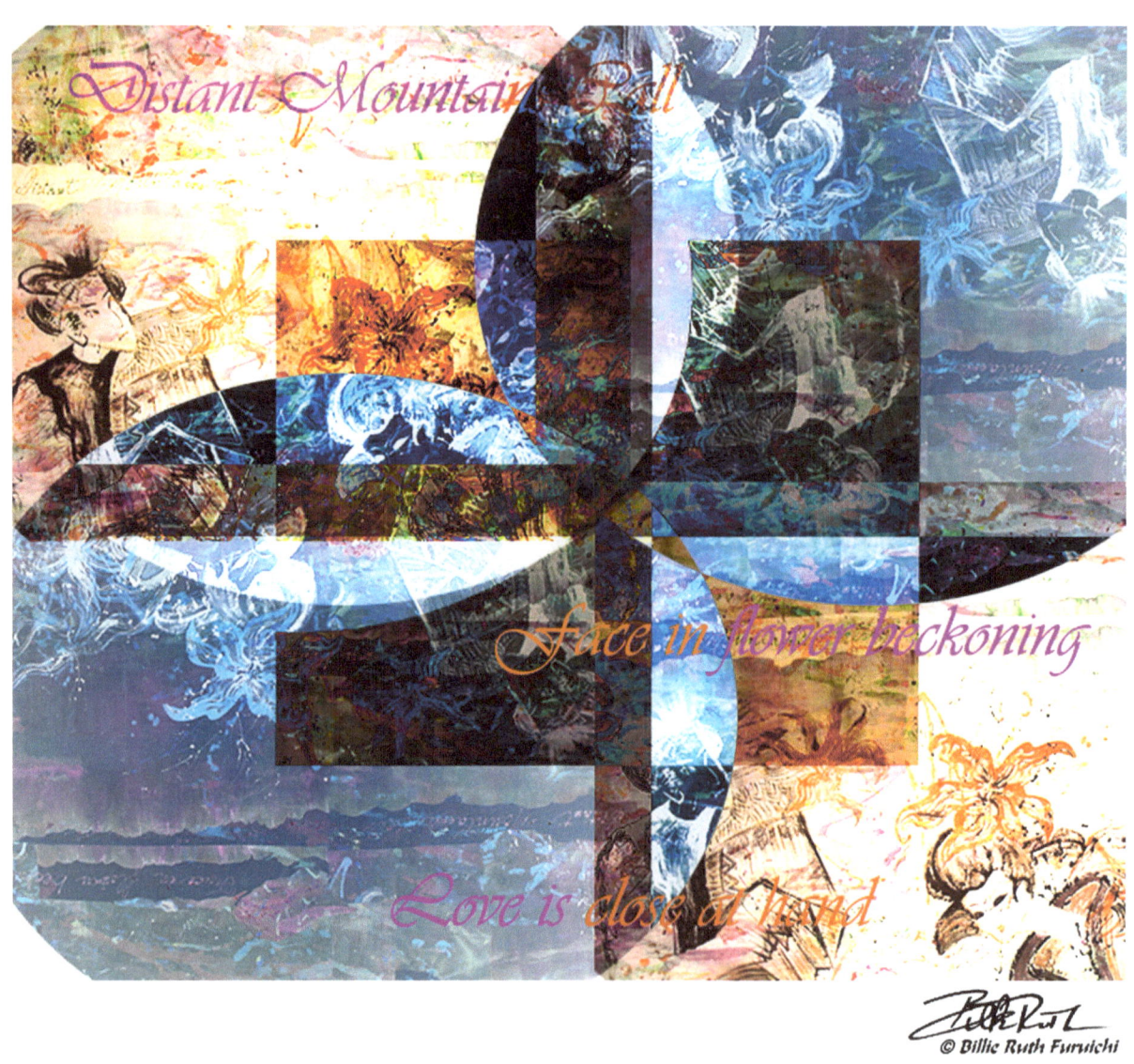

Plate No.14 — Samurai Spirit

Musashi Spirit

Calls across distant
mountains

Otsu waits alone

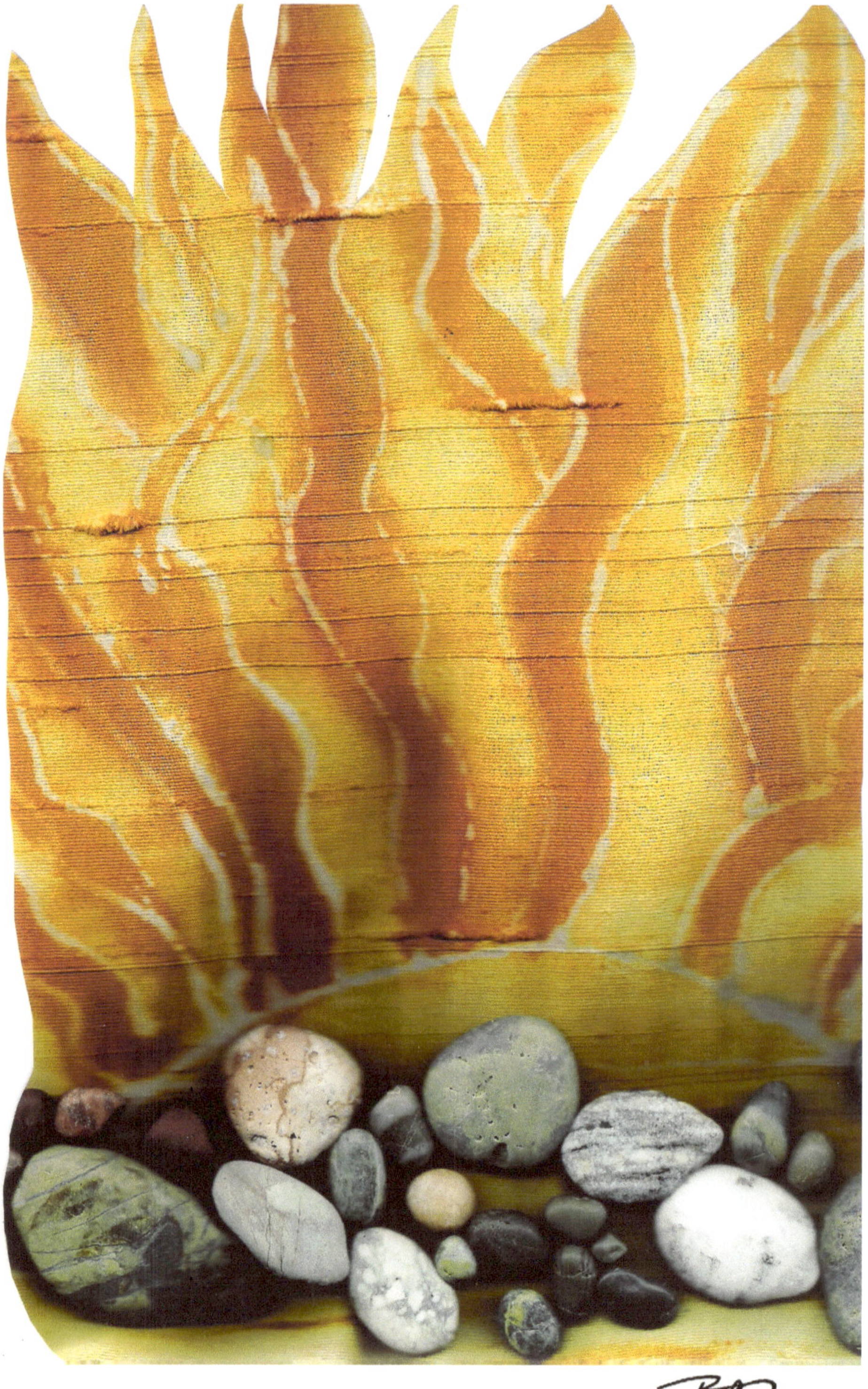

Plate No.15 — Anchoring the Light

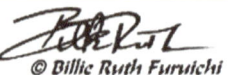
© Billie Ruth Furuichi

Anchoring the Light

Moving on a higher path

Find a secret place

COMMENTARY TWO

ON FEELING THE POWER

On my many trips to Russia, I often stood in front of majestic religious paintings or icons, feeling the living spirit, holy energy, literally pouring through me. If we had been allowed to touch them, we would have all been brought to our knees by The Divine Power System. Each icon is a living thing. Any work of art done with intention and conviction is a living thing that can be felt by the observer. In fact, any living thing can become a vehicle to send us exactly what we need, if we approach it with reverence and intention. Consider ancient Redwoods. Hugging a tree is not a silly thing to do.

The first time I ever saw someone hug a tree, I was about thirty years old. My choreographer from Mexico, Constanza Hool, had come to visit me in Felton, California. We hadn't seen each other since I danced with her troupe at age nineteen. I took her to the usual tourist places, but when we went to Big Trees Park, we got out of the car and she just stood there staring for a very long time. Then, slowly, she approached one of the Redwoods. Arms lifted in praise. She placed her entire body against the bark, I'll never forget it. She laid her forehead on the tree, stretched her arms as far as they could reach around it, and simply breathed there, for at least five minutes without saying a word. I stood watching in awe.

Later I asked, "Constanza, what were you thinking with the trees?"

"Absolutely nothing, Darling," she replied in her lovely thick accent. "You must not think when you are in the presence of such divinity. You must be simply quiet and grateful that you have been given the honor to be in their company for a short time. The trees are dancing, Billie. They are alive. They talk to you. You are blessed to be here, in the presence of such grace and power. Promise me you will go and dance with the trees every day, Billie. They will teach you everything you need to know."

I understood what she was talking about, but in a marriage that could not embrace who I was, and although Constanza taught me more than dancing, it took years before I learned how to drop gravity, send my breath through every cell and particle as I danced, making connection with everyone in the room, while at the same time being lifted so far above myself I was connecting with the outer galaxy. That kind of thing takes more than just a few years.

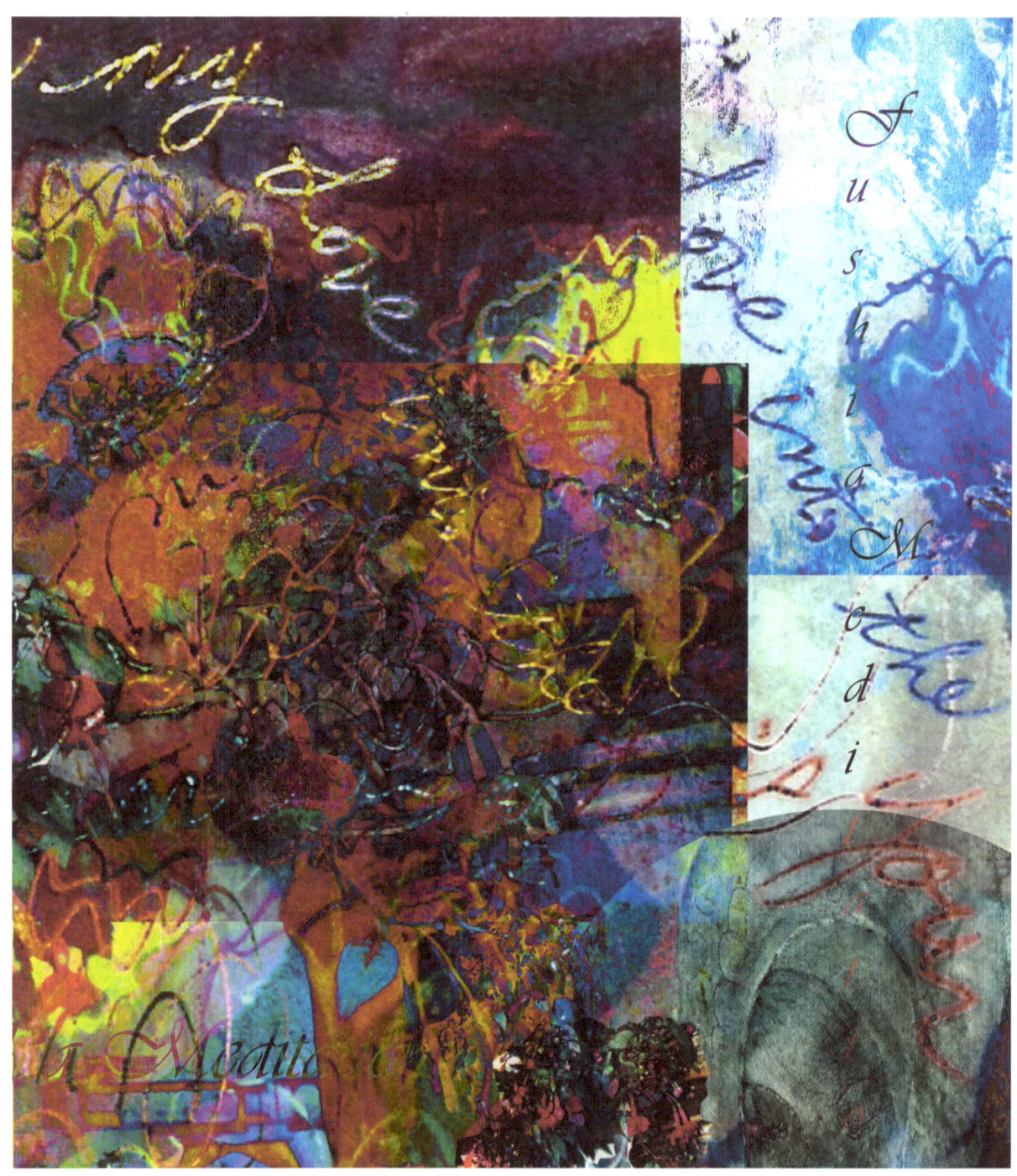

© Billie Ruth Furuichi

Plate No.16 — Inner Vision

Straight on, eye-to-eye

Quantum illumination

Inner Vision source

☯

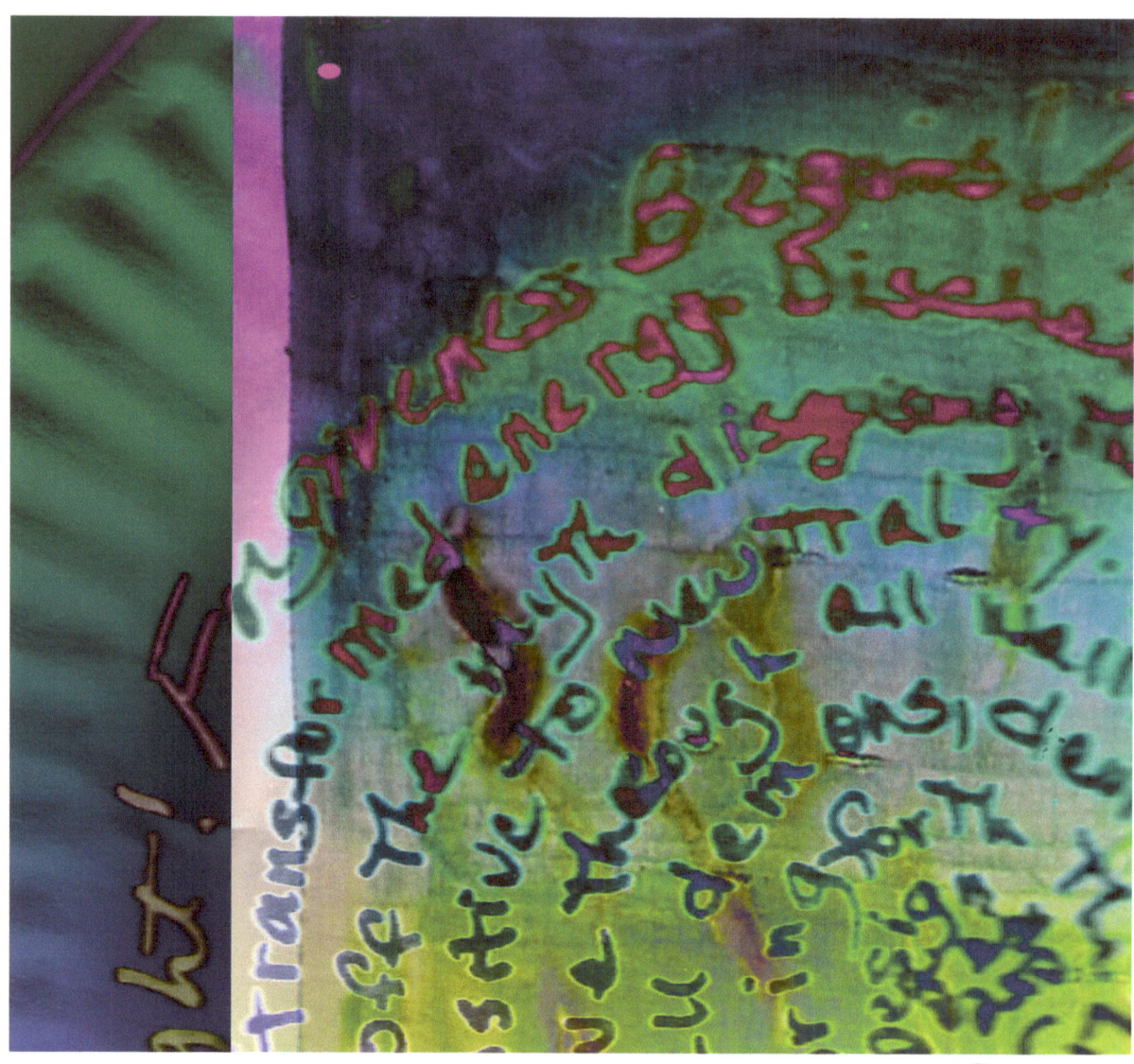

Plate No.17 — Forgiveness Begins

Bands of narrow rings

Ancient tree
      enduring drought

Forgiveness begins

☯

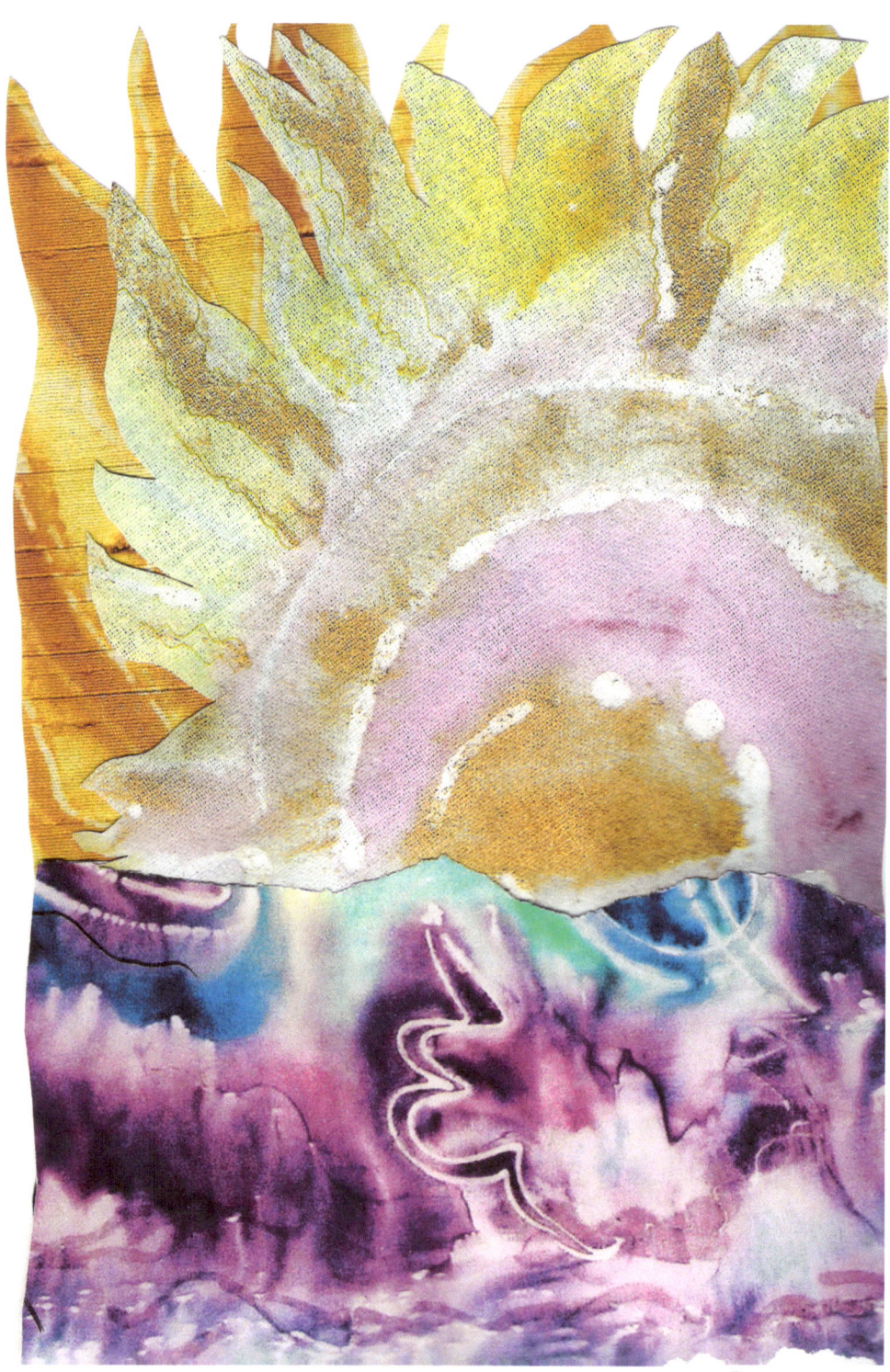

Plate No.18 — Almas Mescladas

© Billie Ruth Furuichi

Somos las guapas

Antiguas del mar y sol

Almas mescladas

☯

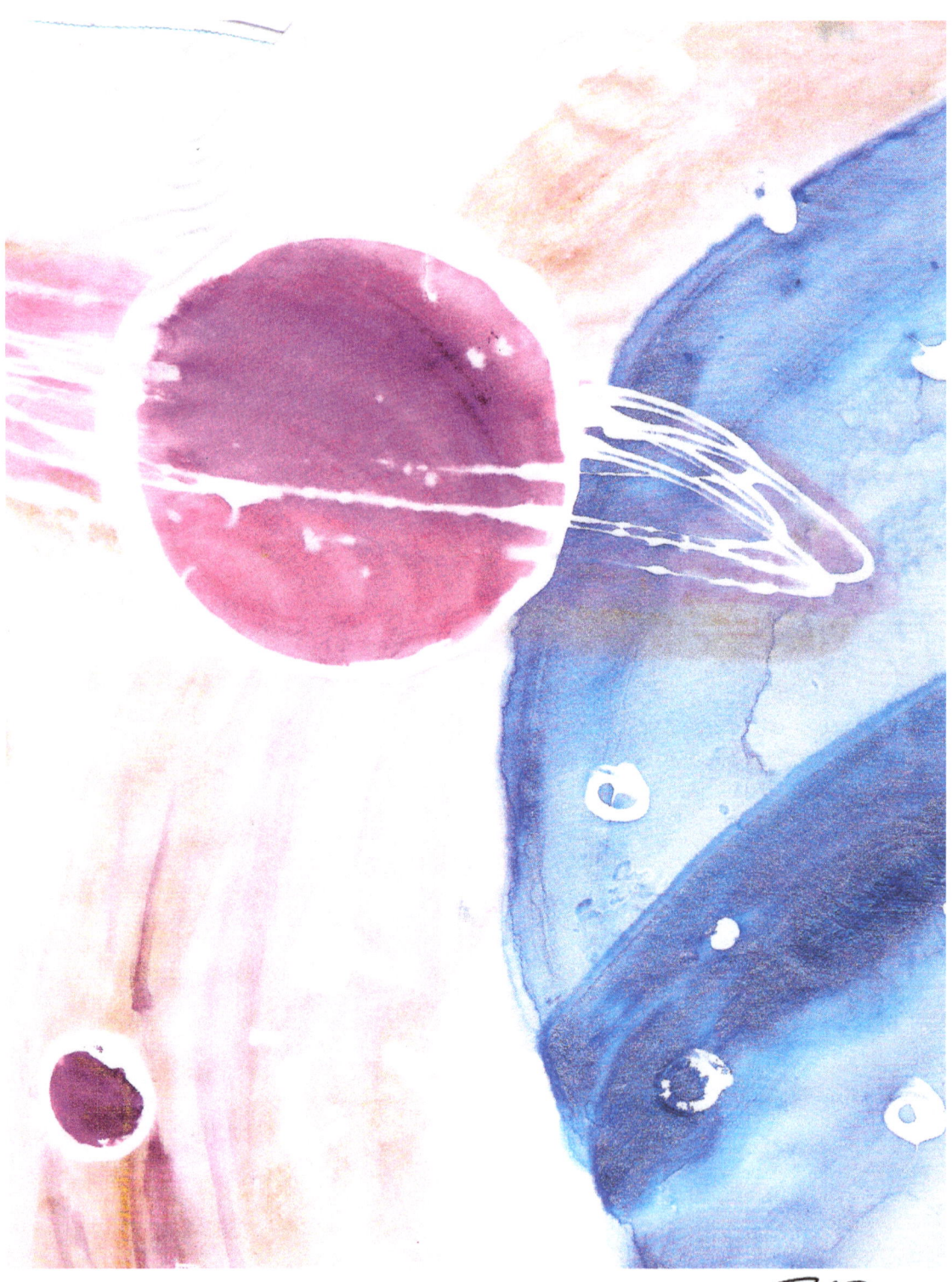

Plate No.19 — Singularity

Mystery revealed

The theory of Everything

Gravity is God

☯

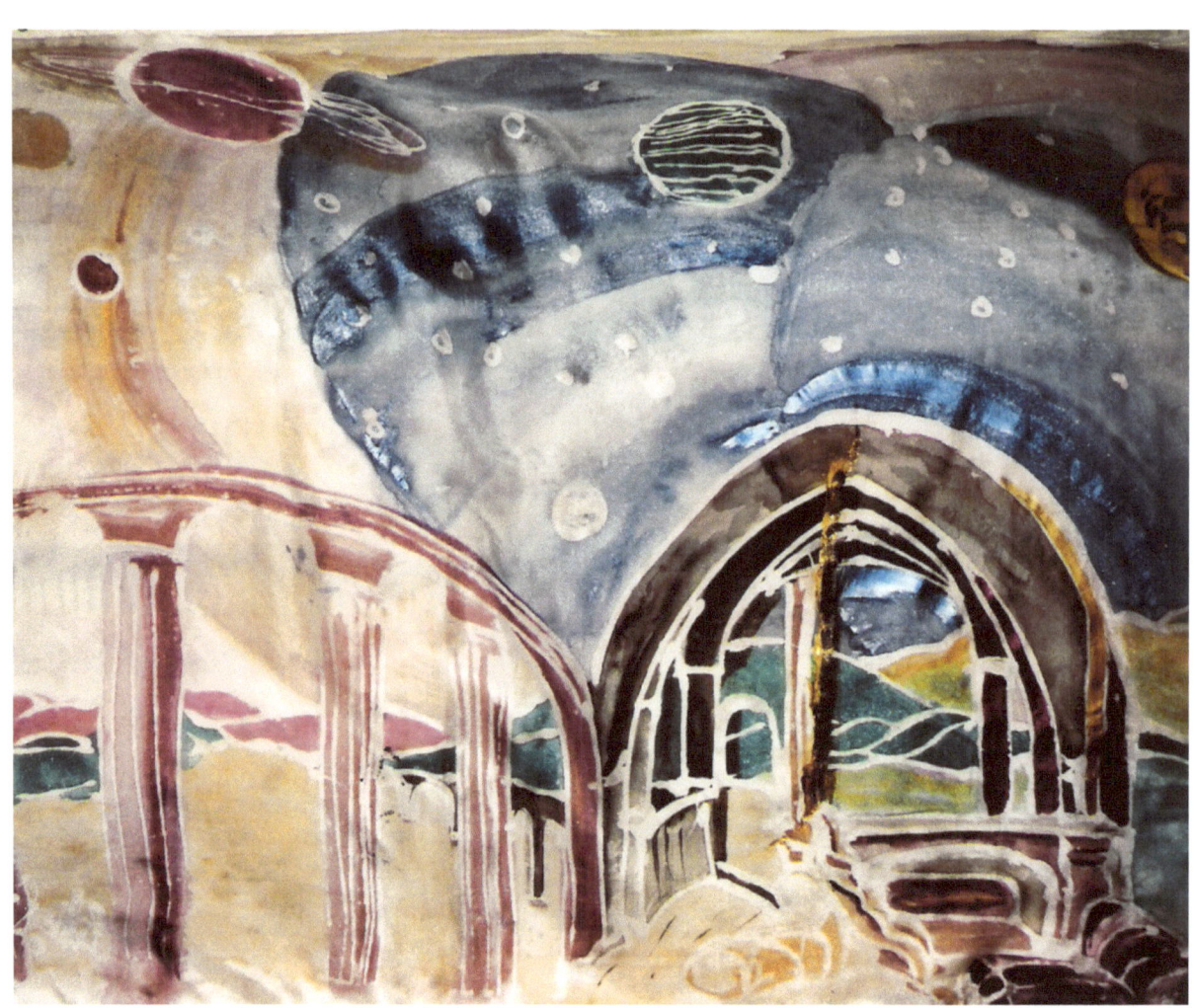

© Billie Ruth Furuichi

Plate No.20 — Crumbling Cathedrals

Once a place of Truth

Arched cathedrals crumbling

Opening the way

☯

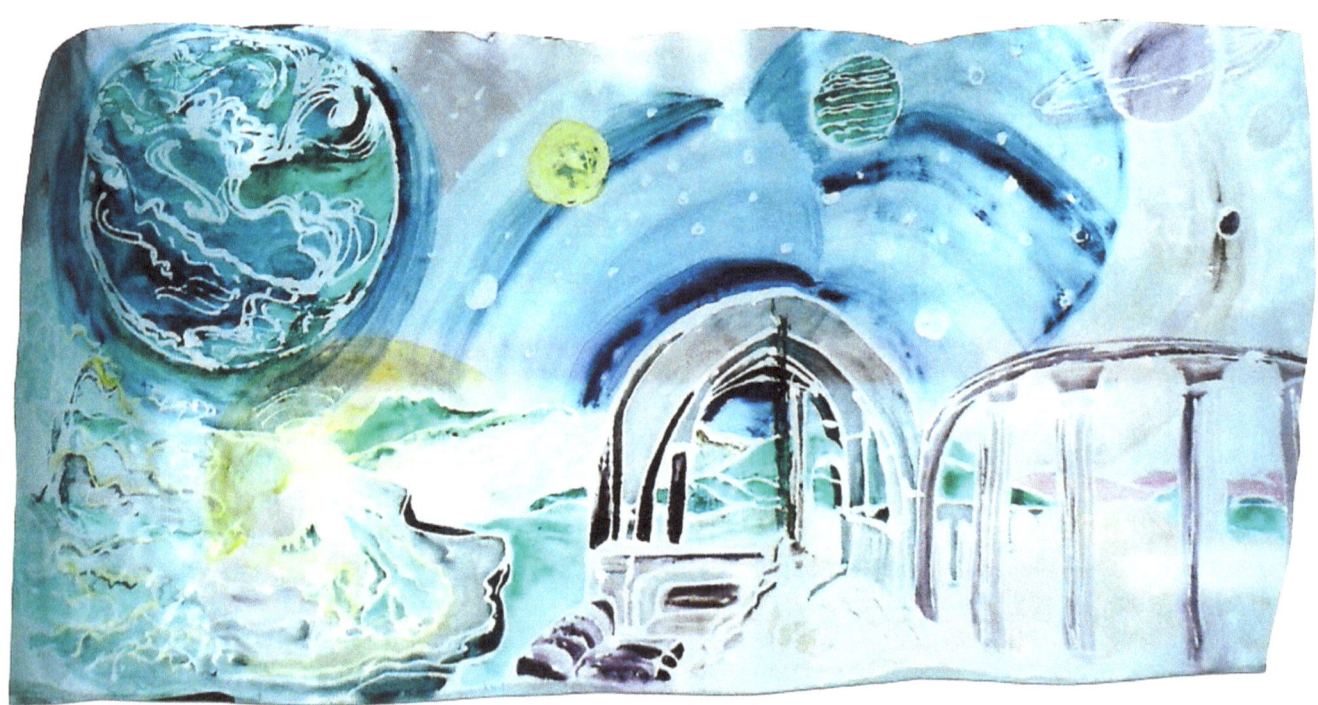

Plate No.21 — Be Ye Not of This World

Connect to the source

Be ye not of this old world

Give thanks and move on

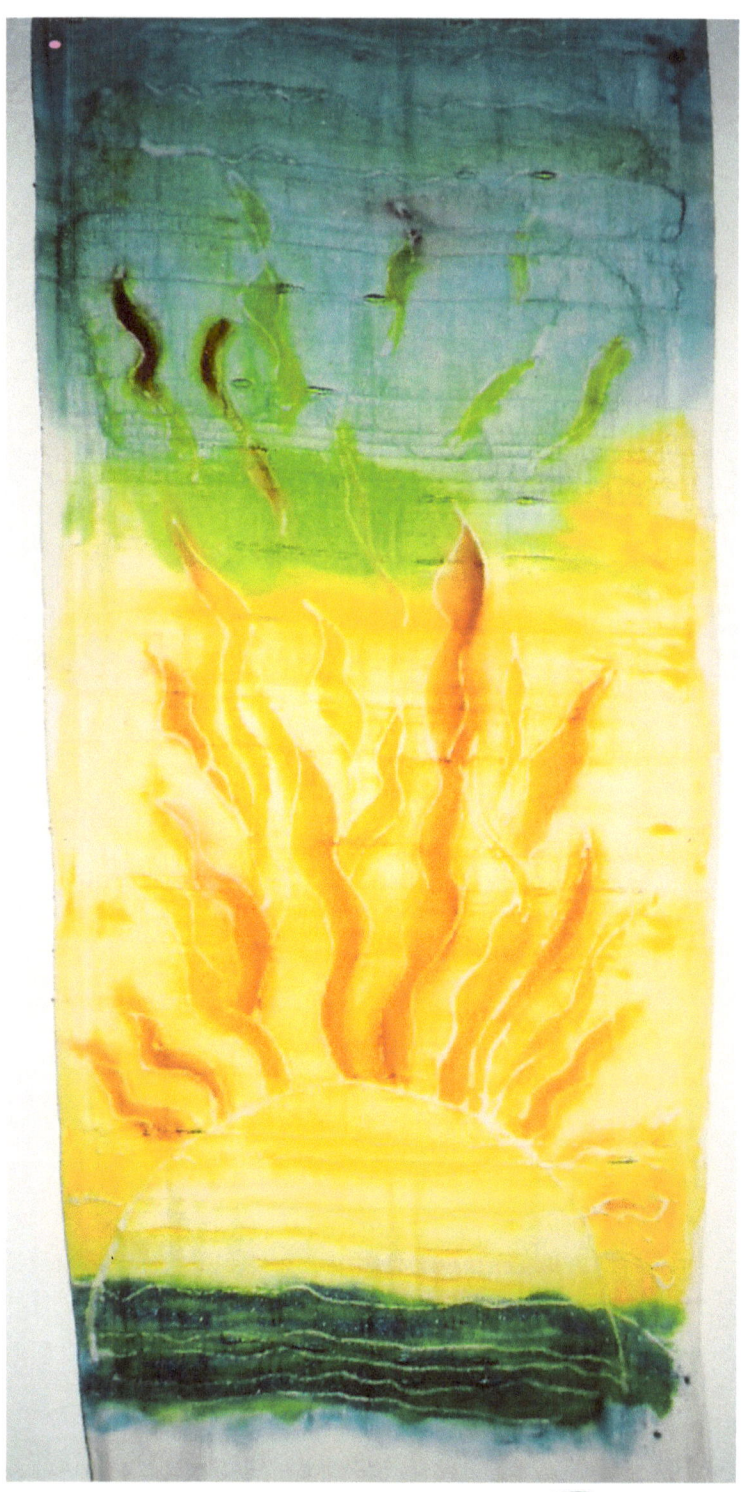

Plate No.22 — Let There Be Light

© Billie Ruth Furuichi

Natural path to source

Surpassing false
                perceptions

Let us anchor Light

☯

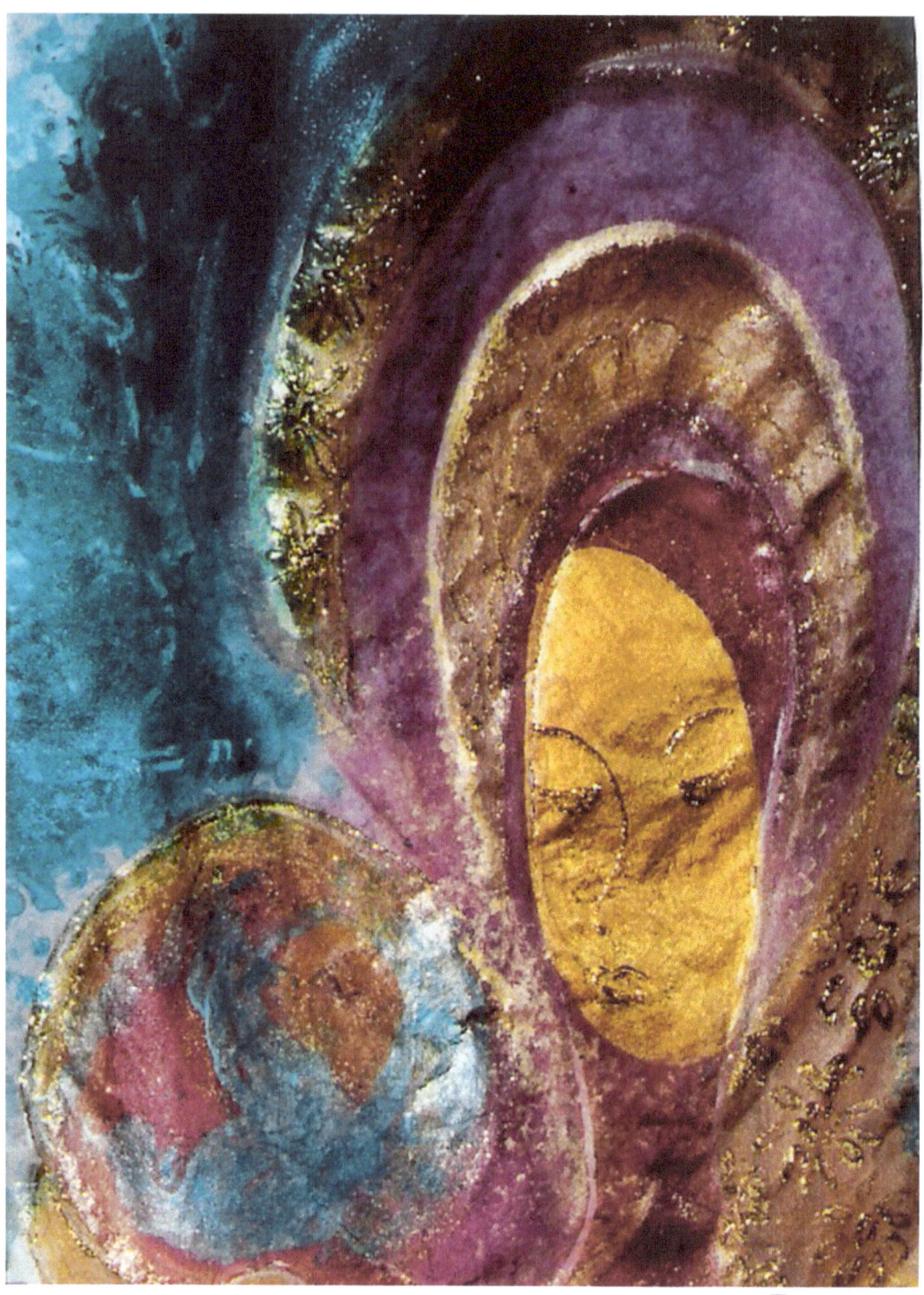

Plate No.23 — Receiving the Child

© Billie Ruth Furuichi

Receiving the child

Mother's breath
　　upon his head

Heartbeats synchronize

COMMENTARY THREE

ON OUR CONNECTEDNESS TO ALL THINGS

Incorporating practices in movement meditation, toning, haiku and silk painting, merge to release and express our deepest creative creatures. This in turn, enables a connection to the Divine. The workshops and seminars I have developed over the past twenty years draw on indigenous motifs locked in our DNA and expressed throughout history as icons, art, artifacts, music, design, myth, religion, etc. I believe these motifs to be interwoven into the very fabric of our lives, expressed in myriad forms, as an intricate web of the mundane and the mystical. Jesus told us we would do even greater works than he did, and I believe him, but our first task is to learn how to discharge our own inner demons so that we can all live in harmony with each other. Chief Seattle said, "What we do to the web, we do to each other." Gandhi said, "Be the change you want to see." All are powerful mandates to help us usher in a new paradigm for our world, but it begins in our deepest inner selves. For me, the first step is to truly model the Divine energy that created me – in that process, I am illuminating the mundane, just as holiday lights on a tree, transform it into a symbol for new life.

Sometimes we could all use a new life. A gift of grace. A second chance. I think it starts through an authentic audience with the Divine, in a private booth in some Secret Place Most High – where we can go to recharge, listen, do our dance of redemption, and sometimes get lucky enough to help transform the world. We can access this connection in a myriad of ways by opening our eyes and recognizing our essential oneness with all things and carrying that awareness with us daily, whether in dance, art and music, or simply waiting at a stoplight for someone to cross the street. When we recognize ourselves in others and say, "Your cause is my cause" there is hope for all life on this planet. Empathy for all precious creatures is essential – the wolf as he jockeys for pack position and howls at the full moon; the dolphin as she nudges her baby upward toward air and leaps in the wake of sail boats for the sheer joy of it, the whale, the polar bear, and so many others for whom we are responsible. The truth is, none is expendable. The degree to which that Truth is actualized, will be the touchstone for future generations. I pray that subsequent generations will still be here to see themselves in the intricate patterns woven by us, and that they may be the web weavers of a viable, empathetic, positive, and peaceful future.

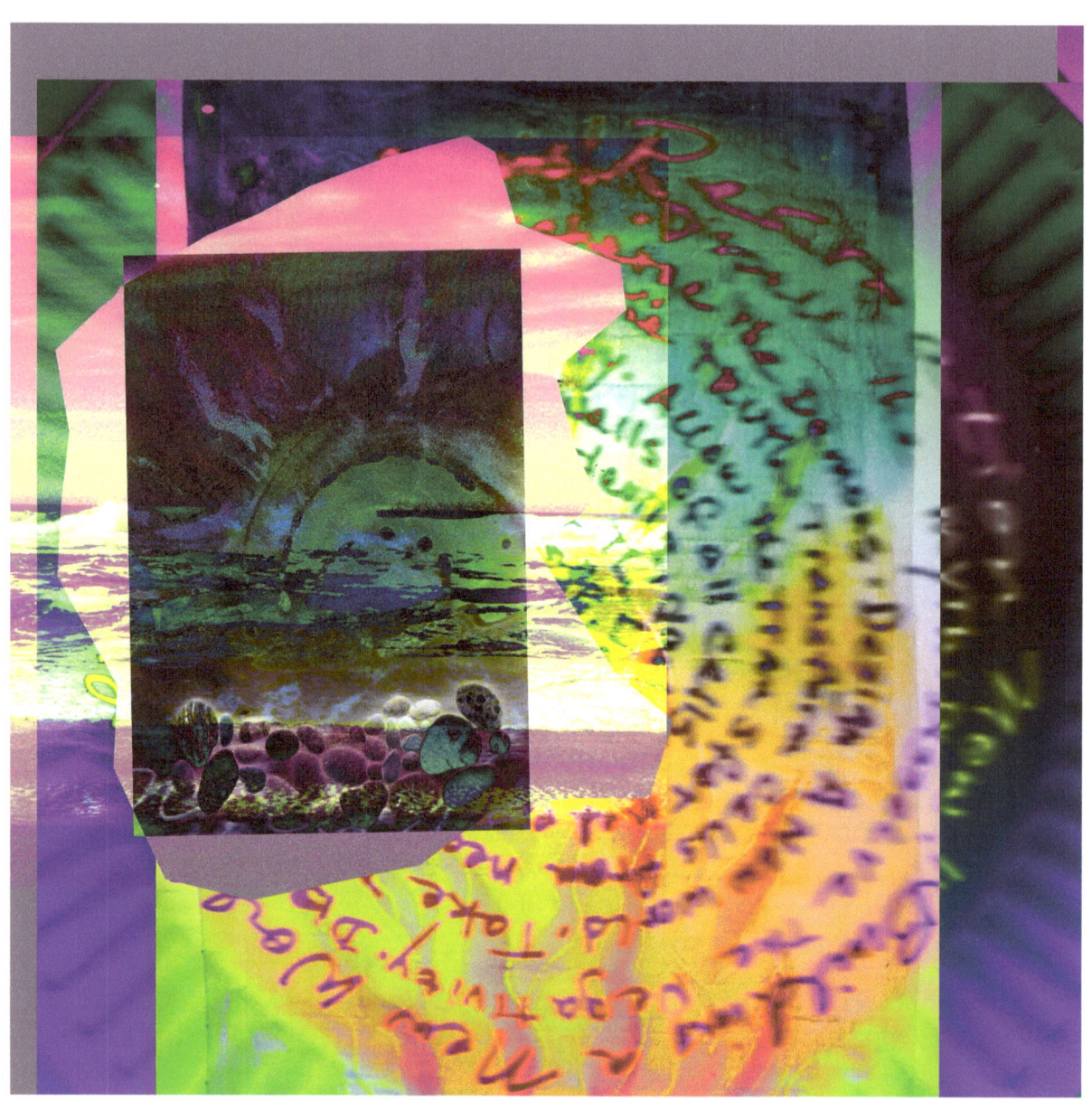

© Billie Ruth Furuichi

Plate No.24 — Sunstones Unlocked

Sun Stones unlocking

Slow deep shift
　　　finding its way

Breath will realign

☯

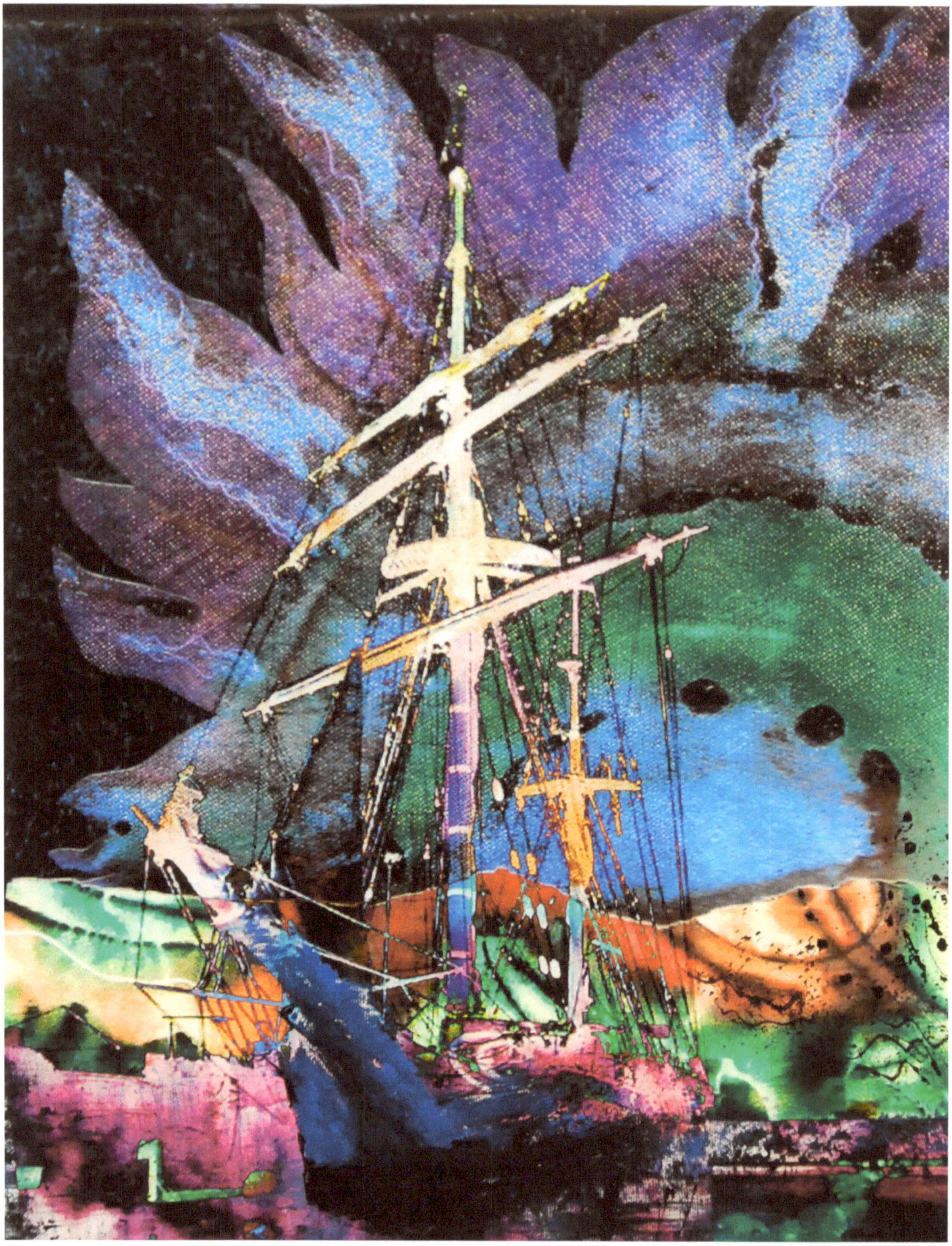

Plate No.25 — Our Lady of Light

© Billie Ruth Furuichi

Our Lady of Light

St. Elmo's fire at her mast

North Star soon appears

☯

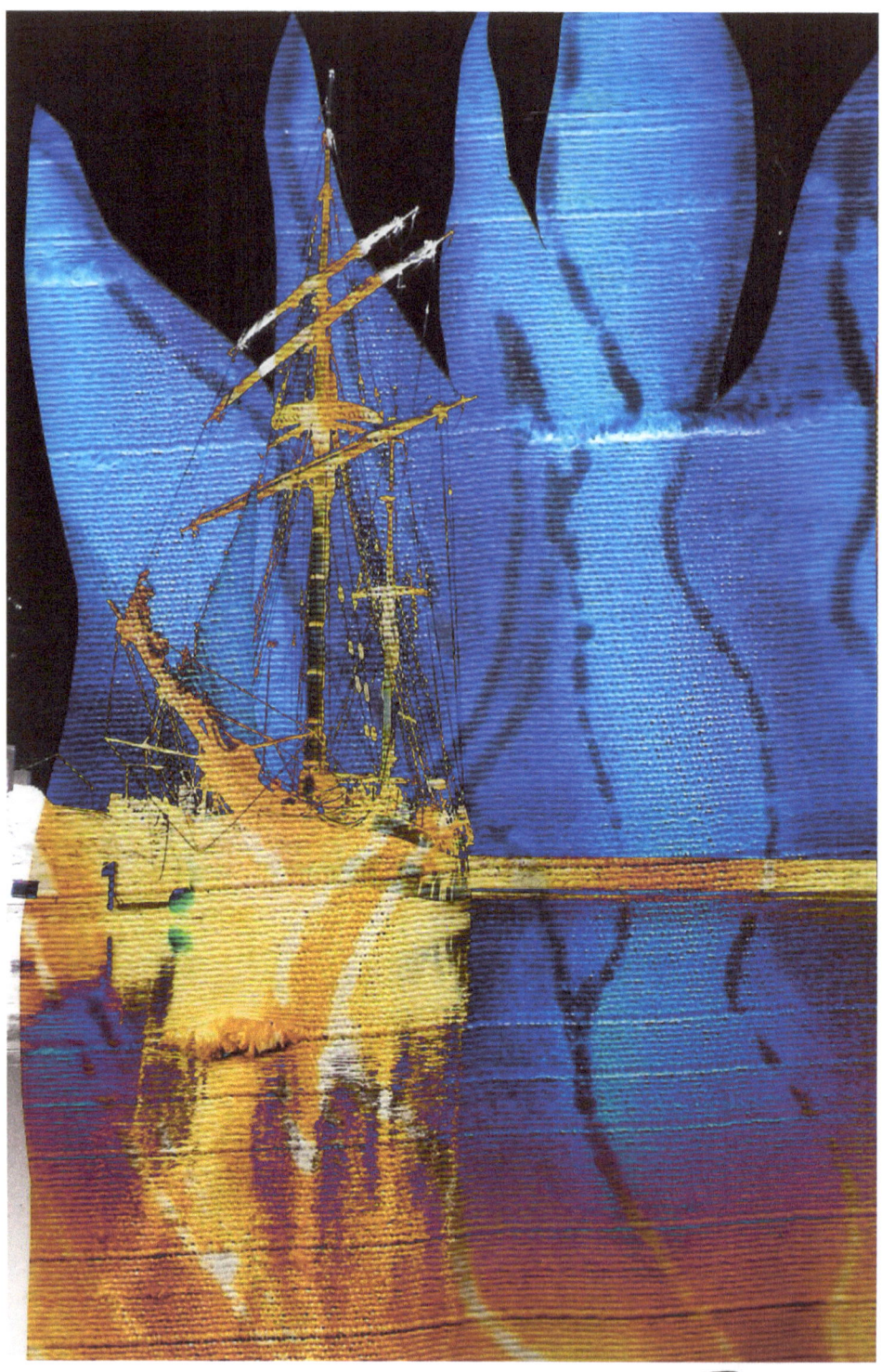

Plate No.26 — Ghost Ship Blue

© Billie Ruth Furuichi

Ghost Ship heading home

Guided by the setting sun

Suddenly she's gone

☯

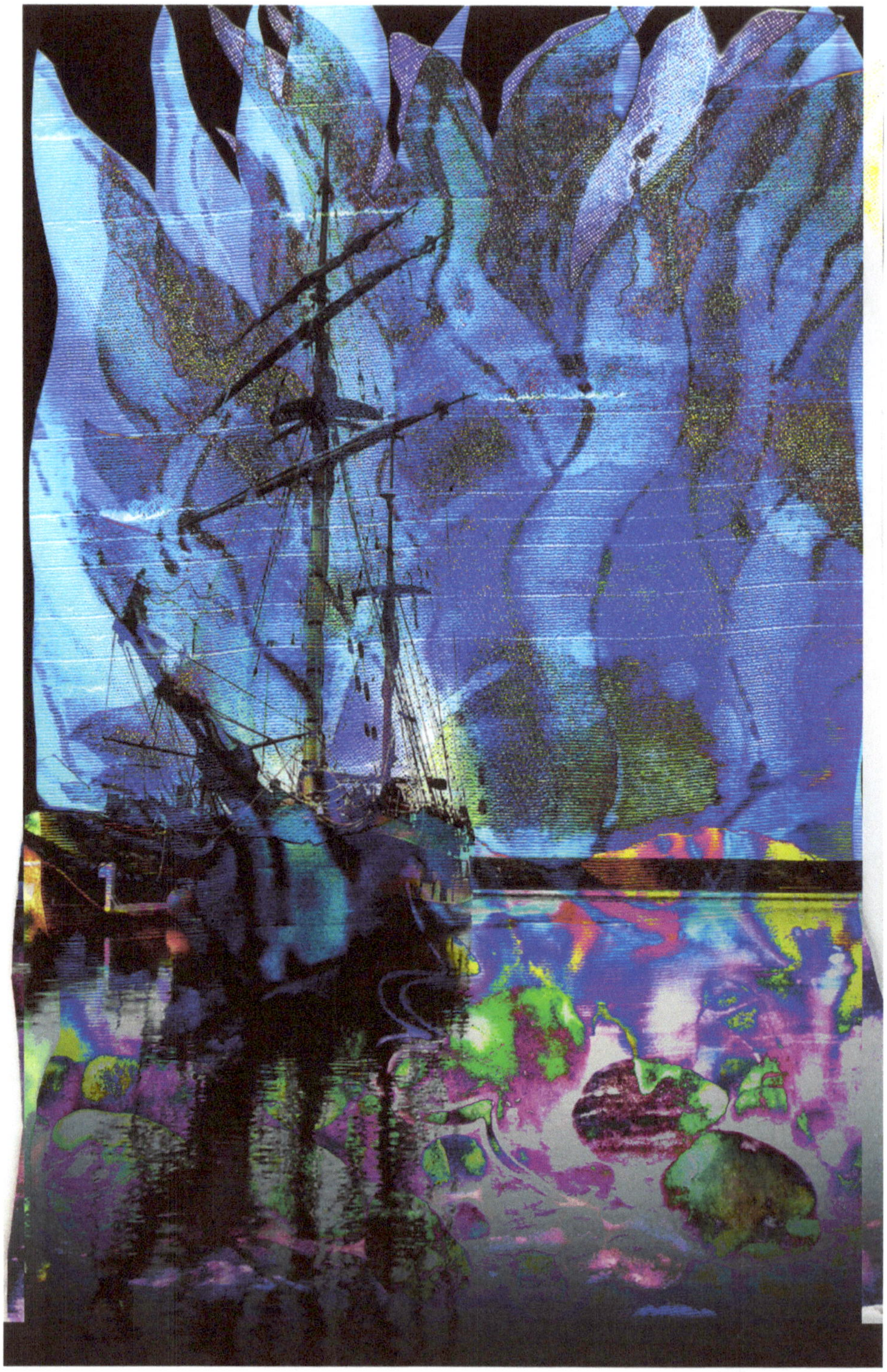

Plate No.27 — Ghost Ship on the Rocks

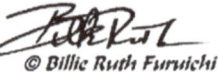
© Billie Ruth Furuichi

61

Ghost ship on the rocks

Yesterday morning's
red sky

Captain did not heed

☯

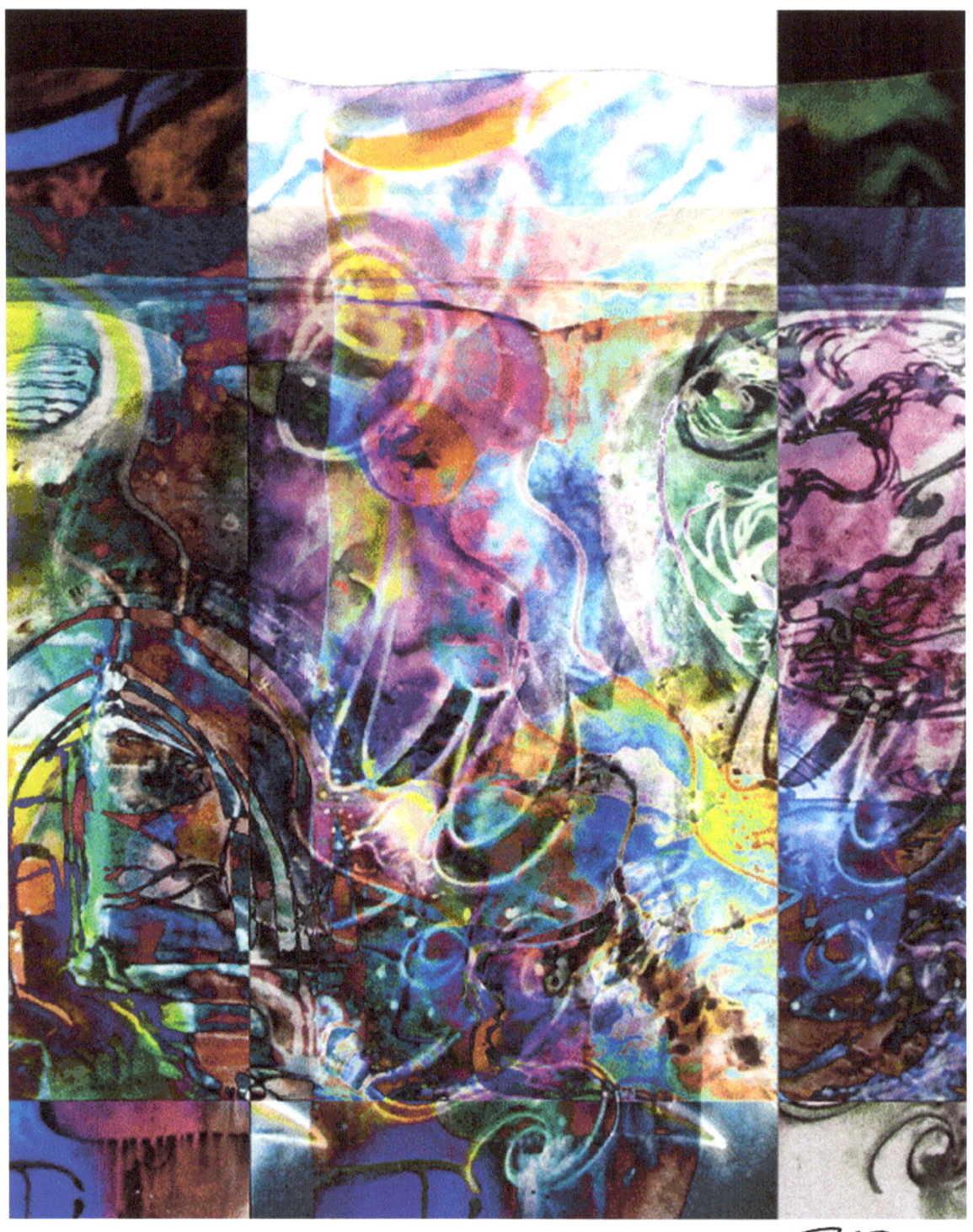

Plate No.28 — Resurrection

© Billie Ruth Furuichi

Find a secret place

Monotheanimism

Resurrection begins

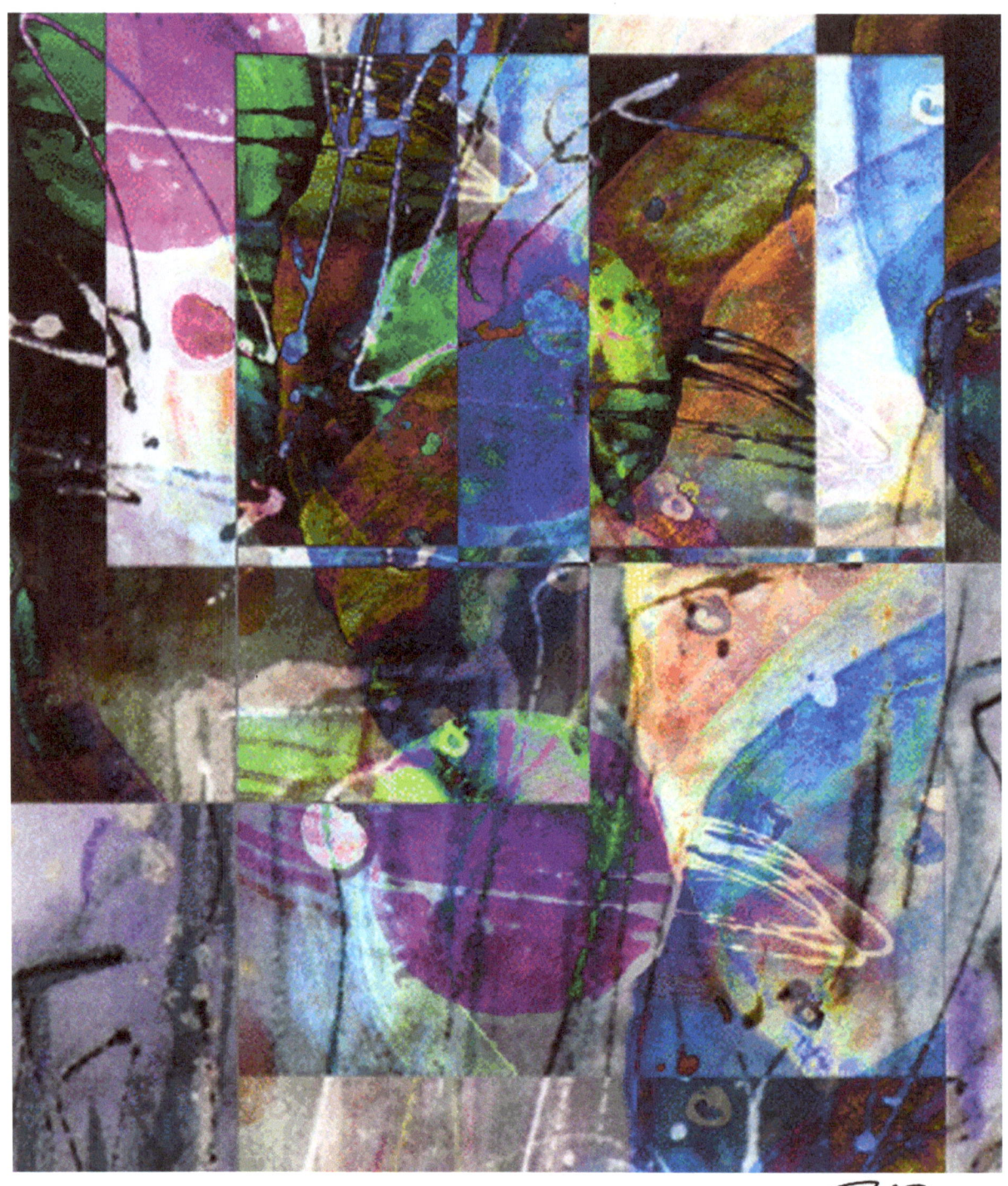

© Billie Ruth Furuichi

Plate No.29 — Through a Glass, Darkly

Through a glass, darkly

Face of moon on lotus pad

Showing me the way

☯

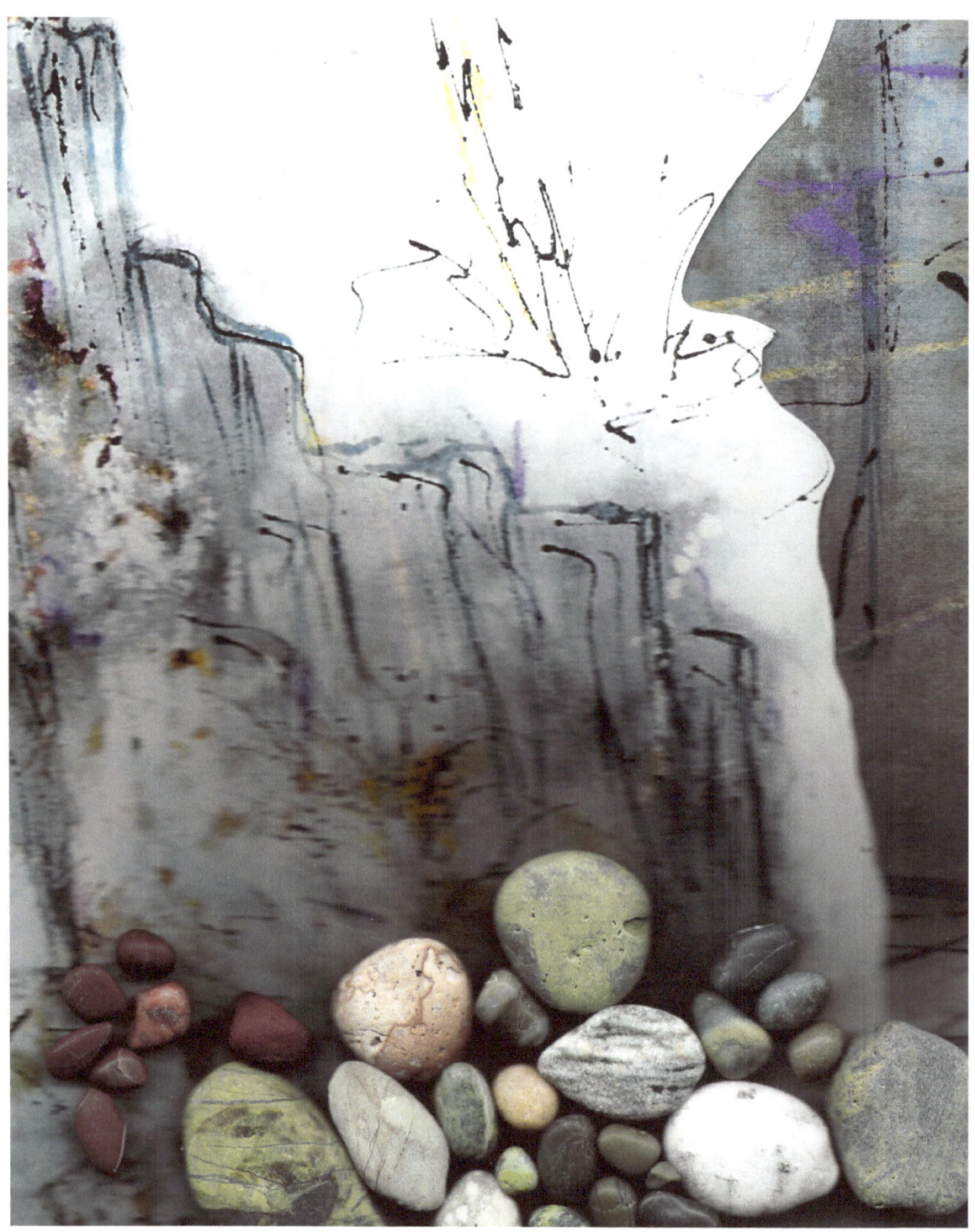

Plate No.30 — Mystical Waters

© Billie Ruth Furuichi

Mystical Waters

Glancing off rocky cliff side

Dance a path to source

COMMENTARY FOUR

ON THE MICRO AND THE MACRO

As a dancer, it is natural for me to integrate movement meditation as a warm-up into a certain mood before painting. My design motifs also naturally take on the style of music I select. When I facilitate a silk painting and movement meditation workshop, I use an adapted version of Rudolph Laban's *movement vocabulary* to help participants visualize design lines and brush strokes. Words like sweep, flow, dab, leap, swirl, wiggle, have perfect visual counterparts for how you want to use the paintbrush as an extension of your body and arms. These words and their design motifs help students produce something beautiful in silk.

During workshops, I also use the Transformation Wheel™, as a tangible channel from this physical world into the spiritual world of the collective consciousness as it relates to the latest theories in Quantum physics. I believe that all life is evolving into and through its present manifestation, as a combined result of the movement and interaction of conscious, decisive, collective, and co-creative energies transforming into quantum atomic forms, evolving from the collective consciousness. Human beings have always created art, artifact, song and dance, mirroring the collective pool of human experience. The old *Does art mirror life, or does life mirror art?* question is still a good one. Maybe it is a bit of both.

But just think about it: Is it possible that conscious, thoughtful, deliberate, positive, spiritual acts of artistic expression can actually produce change in human DNA of both the creator and the observer? I have no idea, but the thought is intriguing and makes for wonderful images in my artwork. When my students and I create silk pieces, I believe they serve as healing icons, not only for us, but for anyone who touches them thoughtfully, with intention to regenerate in some way. This was the intention of ancient religious icons which still contain the energy of the gold and the gemstones that were crushed into the paints the artist used hundred of years ago when they were painted. In much the same way as a medicine wheel, a rosary, or a mandala is a prayer vehicle, The Transformation Wheel™ (a heuristic cognitive/affective device) helps us remember and anchor our realizations.

If other people are anything like me, *Aha moments* and epiphanies can be gone in a flash if we don't document them. My artwork and haiku are my way of documenting realizations from Spirit. One of my pieces, *Gravity, Escaping*, documents a message given to me while walking my dog in 1996 (*We are the spaces between all forms. All forms shall fade. Only We shall abide. Only the spaces shall abide*), but it was not until this year, doodling a Valentine's Day card and thinking about Love, did it all come together. I've held a long time theory that *Love = Gravity = God*. Both Love and Gravity attract us, keep us together, blow us apart, pull us back, anchor us. Love escapes us if we don't take care of it. God's Love will also escape us if we don't take care of it, but it will always be right there waiting for us to retrieve it. Since God IS Love, God must also be Gravity. Scientists can measure all other forces except Gravity, when they smash atoms together. Some think it is escaping into eleven parallel universes. All they really know is that some of it escapes, leaving a yellow shaft of light in the gap where it should be – The Mystery Particle. We might just as well call it God, the Living Spirit of Holy Energy.

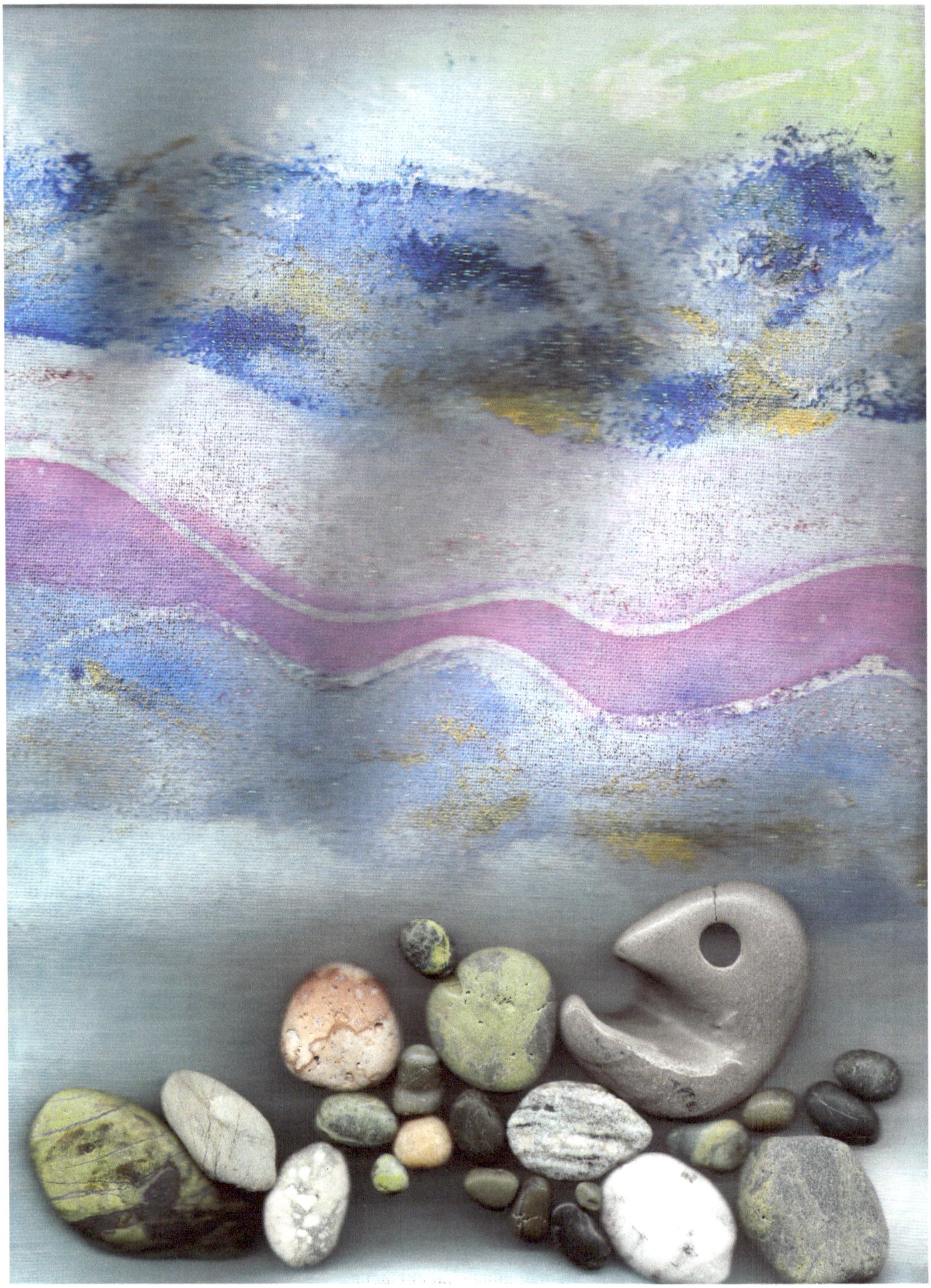

Plate No.31 — Ancient Faces

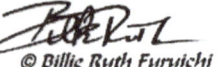
© Billie Ruth Furuichi

Sand and sea wash clean

Universe inside my soul

Ancient face exposed

☯

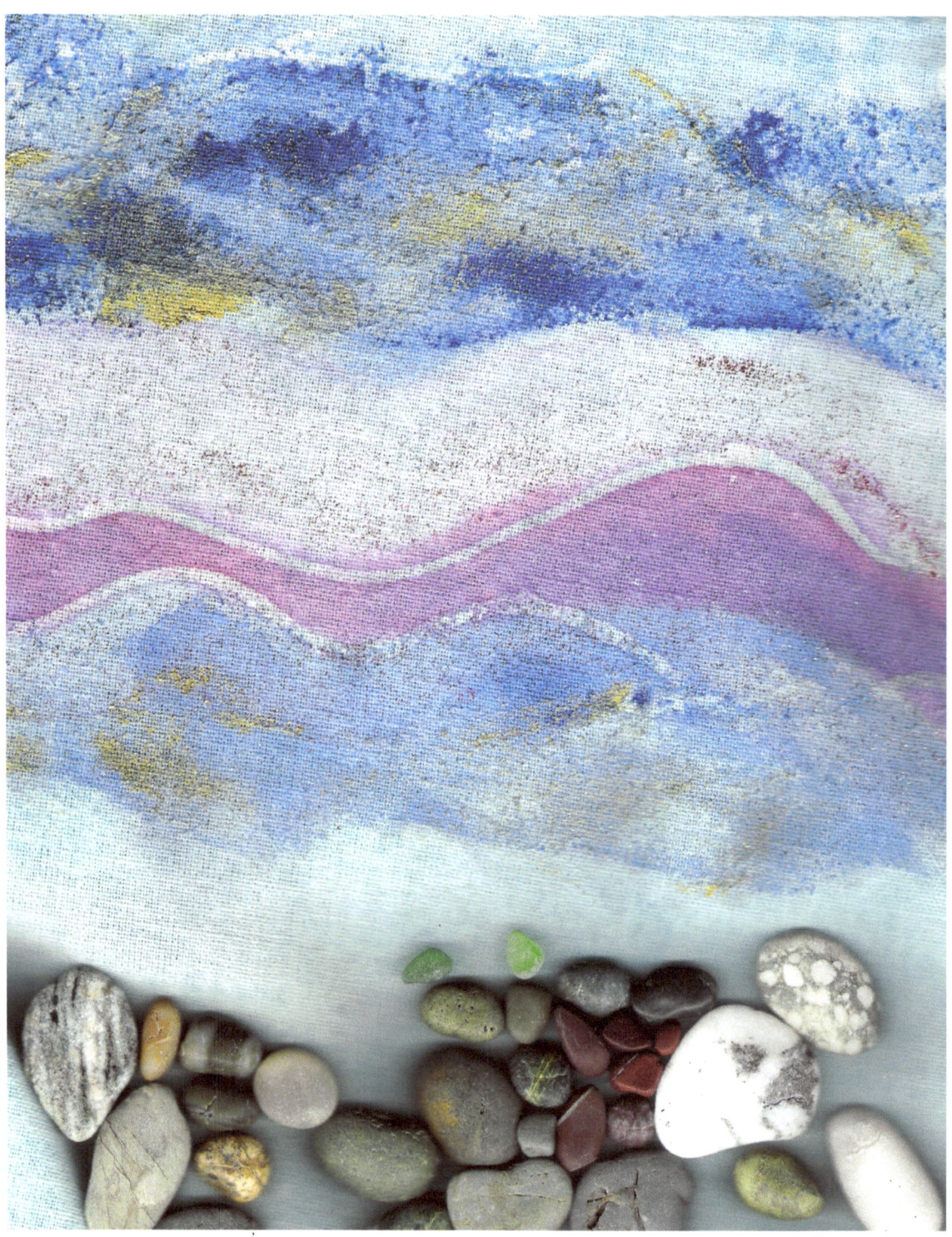

Plate No.32 — Sacred Sea Stones

© Billie Ruth Furuichi

73

Sacred Sea Stones locked

Shimmering in sand and foam

Capsules of past lives

☯

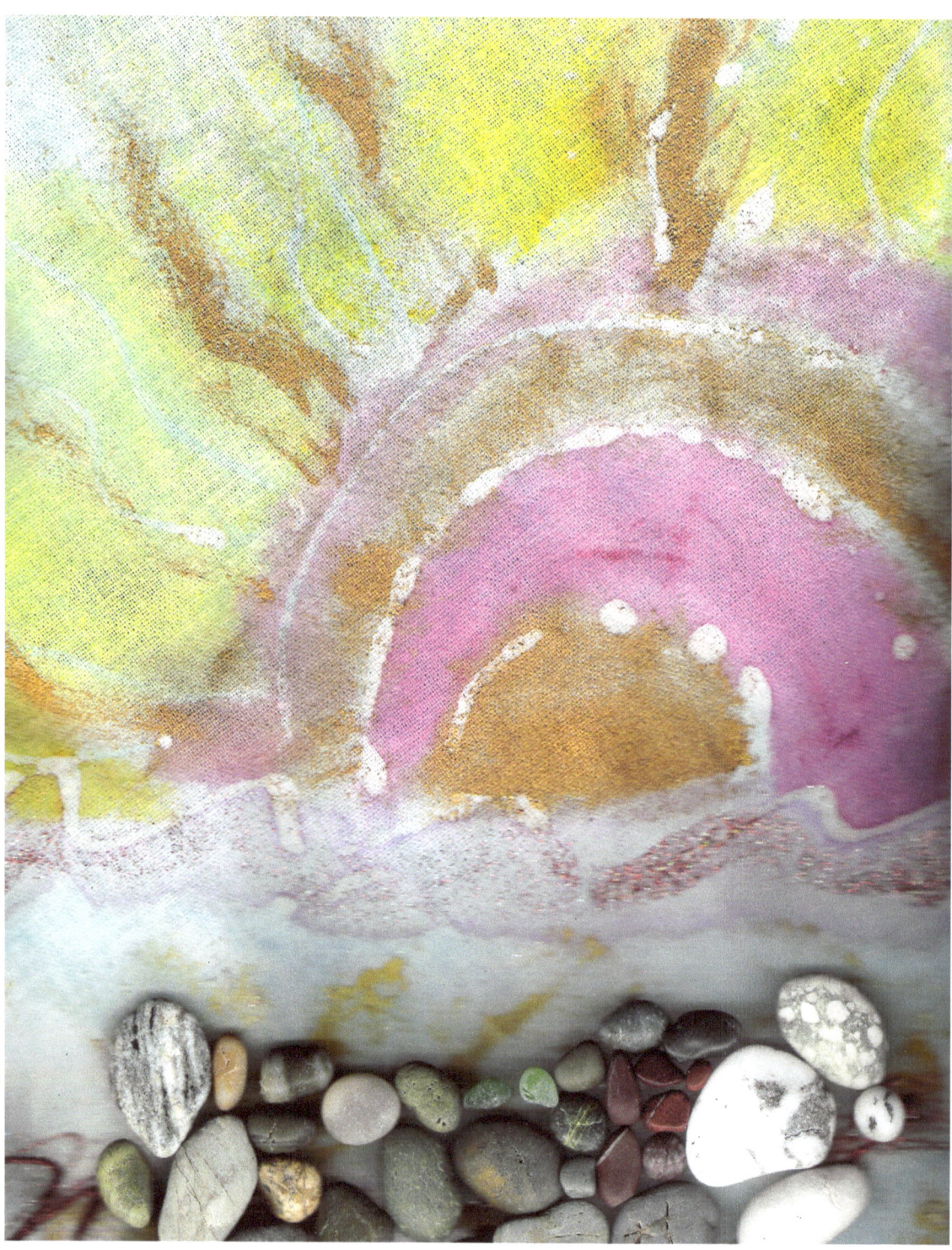

Plate No.43 — Sacred Sun Stones

© Billie Ruth Furuichi

Sacred Sun Stones wait

Patiently until it's time

Polar shift is nigh

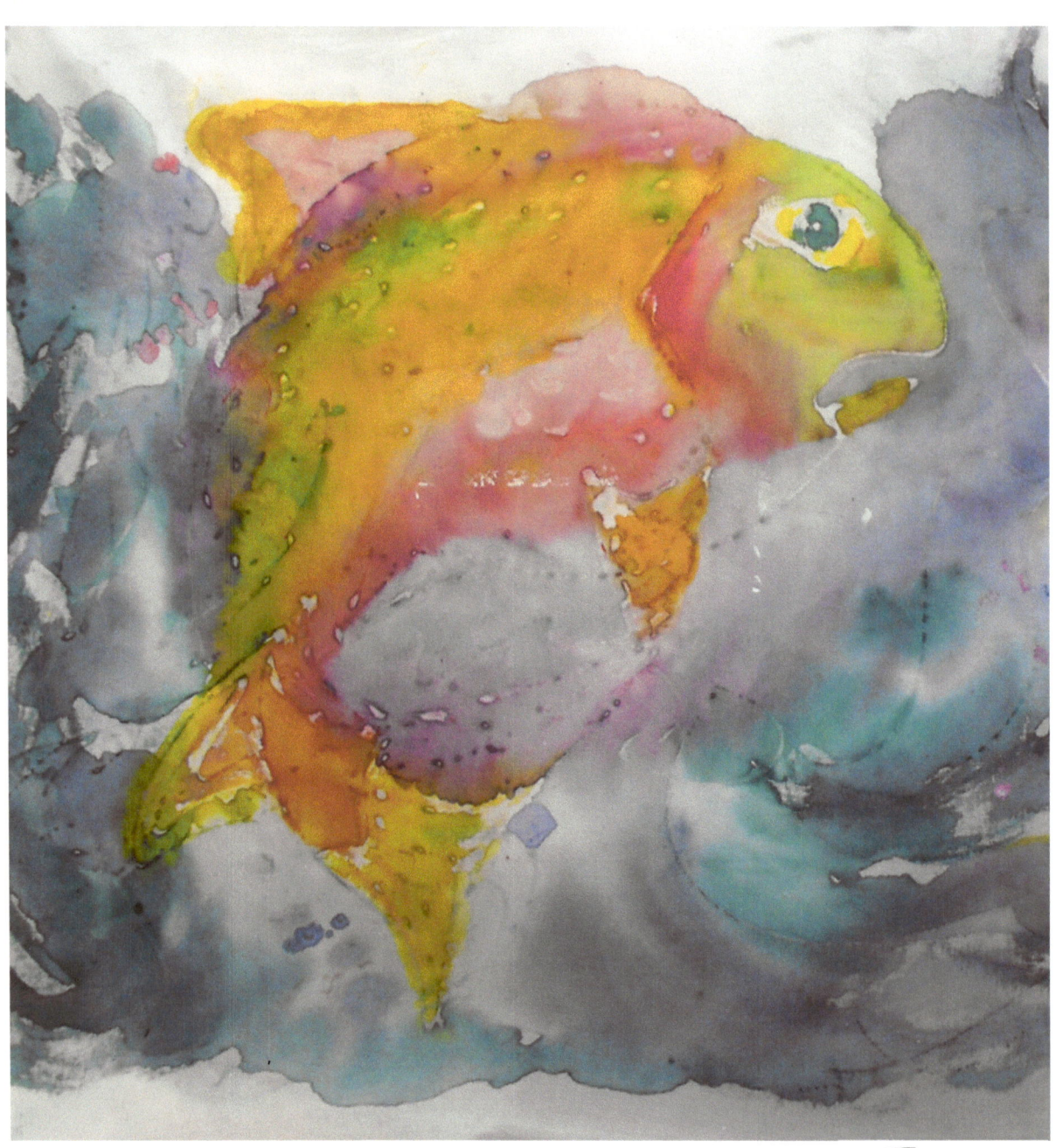

© Billie Ruth Furuichi

Plate No.34 — Wise Fish

Wise Fish heading home

Knowing the way
to his source

New cycles begin

☯

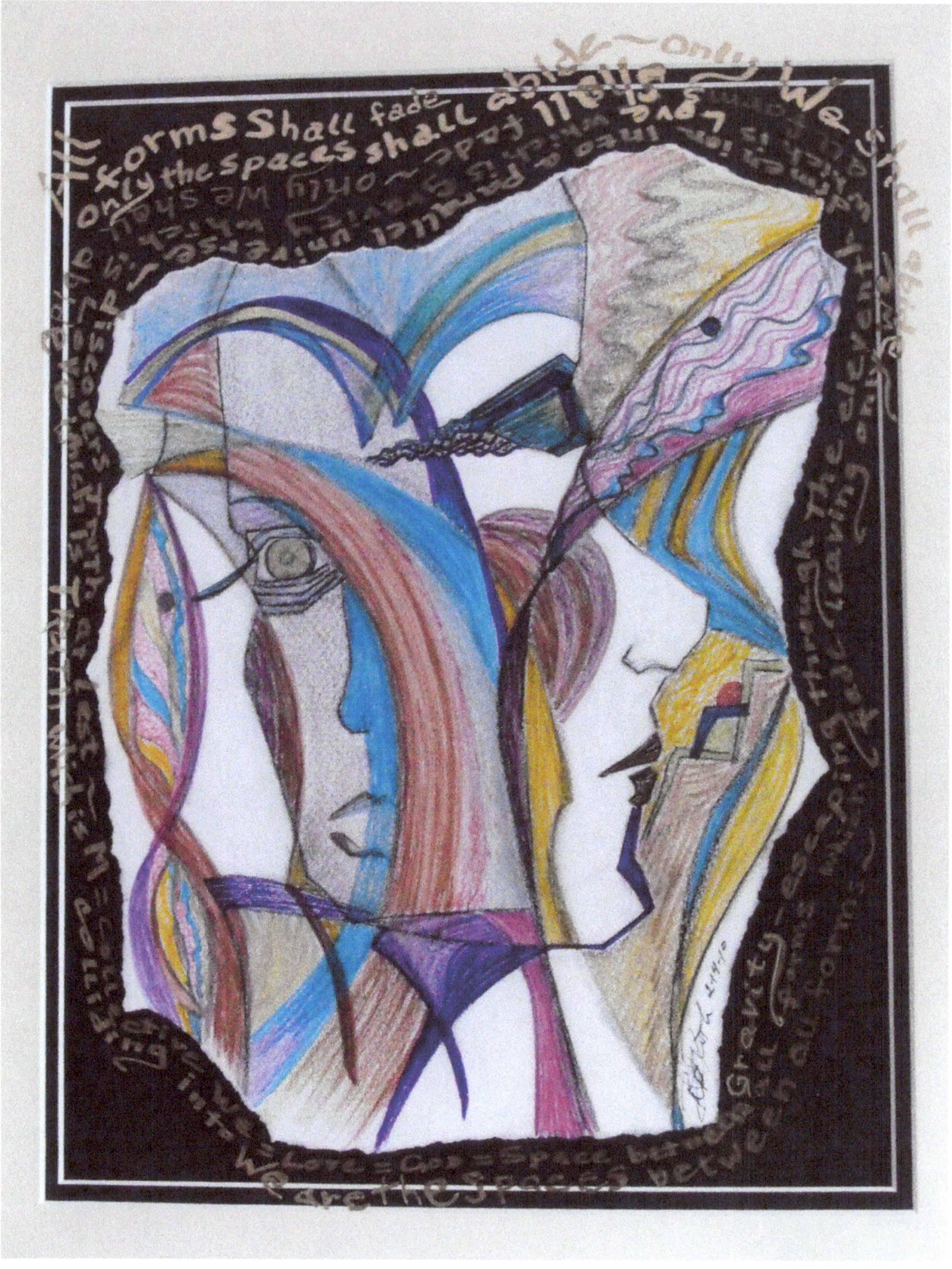

Plate No. 35 — Gravity, Escaping

Gravity escapes

We are spaces in between

Returning as Love

☯

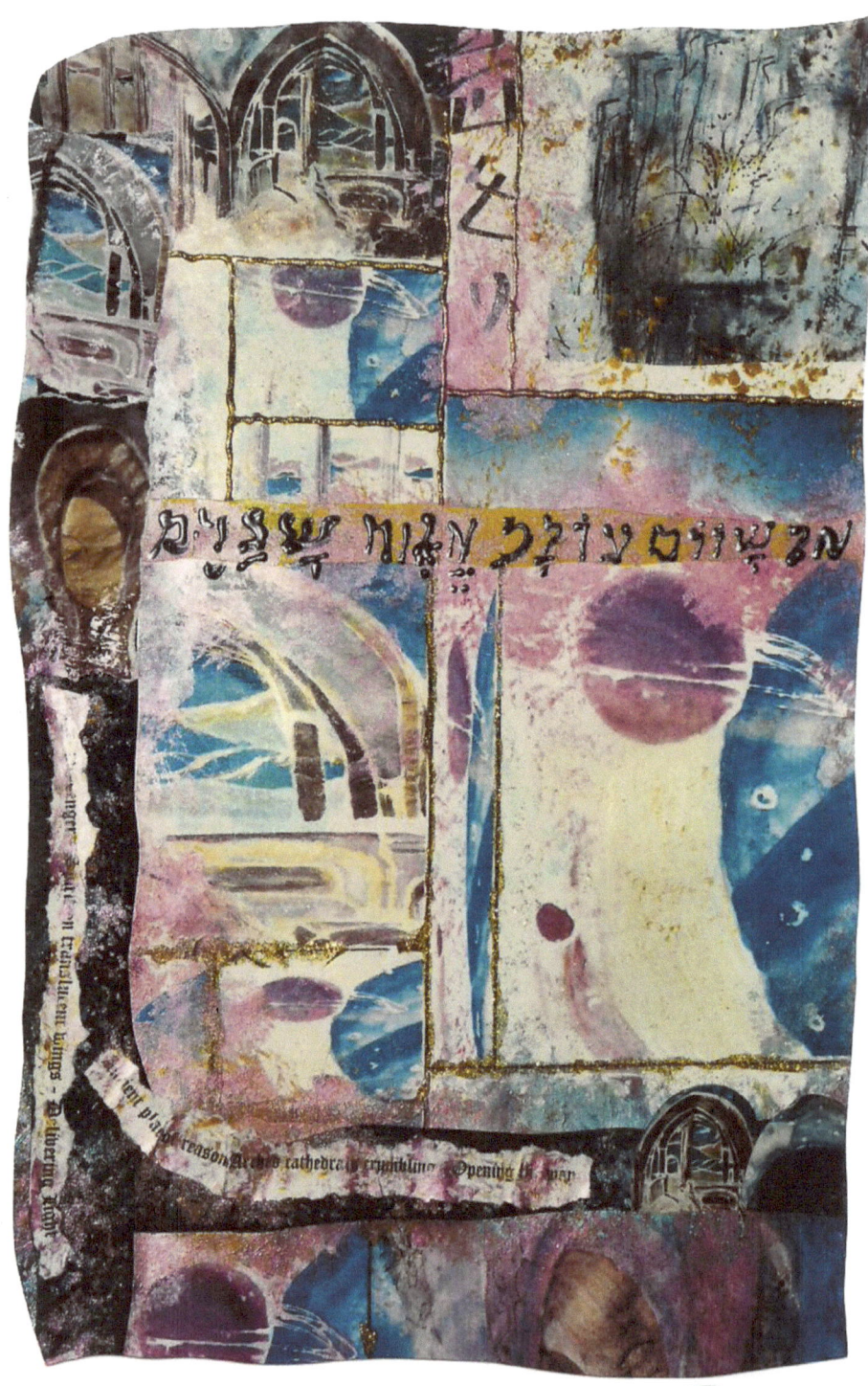

Plate No. 36 — Simultaneous Singularities

Simultaneous

Angel messengers
                whispering

Singularities

☯

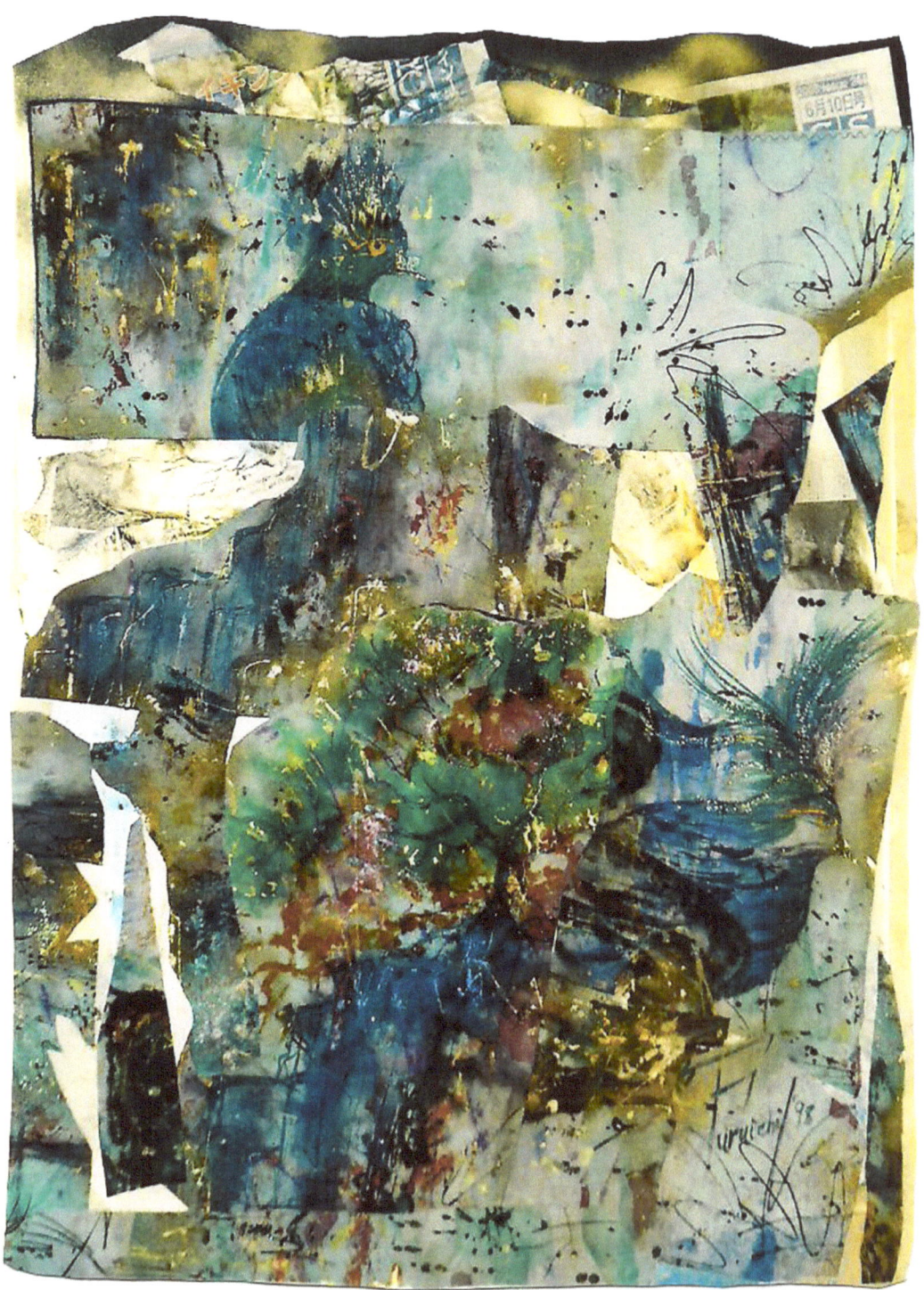

Plate No.37 — Birds in Paradise

© Billie Ruth Furuichi

Birds in Paradise

fly in the face of reason

Angel messengers

☯

The Transformation Wheel®
Board Game

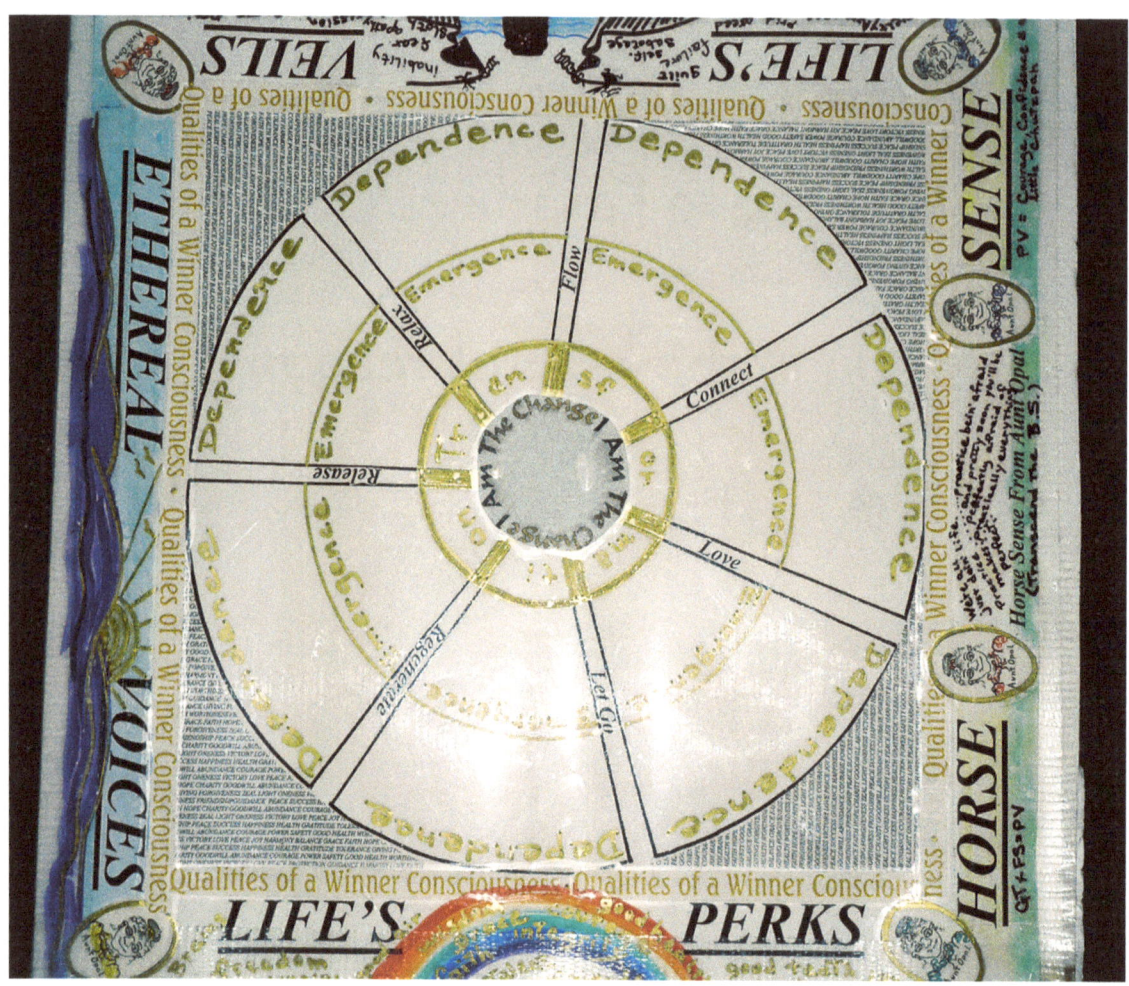

©1993 **The Transformation Wheel® Board Game**

Trained facilitators may become licensed for full use. One time limited permission to use or reprint may be obtained by contacting Billie Ruth Hopkins Furuichi; *anchor35@frontier.com* or www. *furichiarts.com*

ABOUT THE ARTIST

Billie Ruth Hopkins Furuichi has an eclectic background that ranges from acting, singing, dancing, and teaching, to technical training design and development. With an early start in the classics, Billie Ruth studied with Covillo-Parker School of Ballet, Dr. Antonia Brico and Howard Reynolds. Throughout elementary and middle school years, she played violin in the All City Orchestra, and helped her Aunt Ruth teach art at the Children's Art Museum. During high school, Billie Ruth performed as a folk singer, dancer and actor in a variety of professional and summer stock venues. She later traveled to Mexico as a jazz singer and dancer for major TV and stage performances.

After graduating from the University of California in Santa Cruz, and receiving teaching certifications in English and Spanish, Billie Ruth taught high school and performed with the Redwoods Repertory Theatre in Ben Lomond, California. She then spent four years as a technical writer in telephony and microelectronics design. Later, while living on Maui, she developed an original stress-reduction workshop for hotel management. This evolved into a leadership workshop for citizen diplomats and youth ambassador exchanges to the former USSR. In 1990, she founded a non-profit intercultural arts and languge organization, One Society International. OSI conducts Youth-in-Action exchanges from Denver to Japan, under the direction of JoAnne Harada. In 2003, the Colorado Department of Human Services contracted Billie Ruth to develop and facilitate a decision-making and conflict resolution workshop using her Transformation Wheel®, for a group of 50 youth-at-risk, during their annual conference, *A Season of Change*.

Billie's workshop, *Breathing Through Walls*, became the foundation for her most recent workshop, *Anchoring The Light*, integrating music, movement meditation and fabric painting. Billie Ruth has also written and produced a musical fable, *Angelita and The Way of Aethergis*, incorporating decision-making and conflict resolution practices for youth. Billie has a gift for working with young people, inspiring them to reach for and to accomplish their own creative dreams. She is currently launching

Strategic Foresight Expressive Arts Institute in Brookings, Oregon, as an official project of OSI. She also teaches part time for Brookings/Harbor School District.

Bringing grounded educational technology face-to-face with a proactive approach to arts education, using role play, music, dance and painting, Billie Ruth believes we can all make a difference, find ways to "Be the Change" as Gandhi said, and help heal the planet.

Billie Ruth is available for workshops, keynote speaking, and one-day seminars. Her topics include:

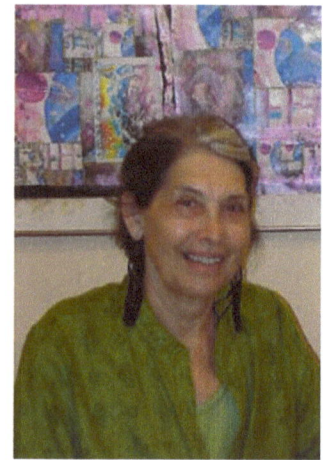

- *Finding Your Peace Wings*

- *Building Bridges of Love*

- *Breathing Through Walls*

- *Anchoring The Light*

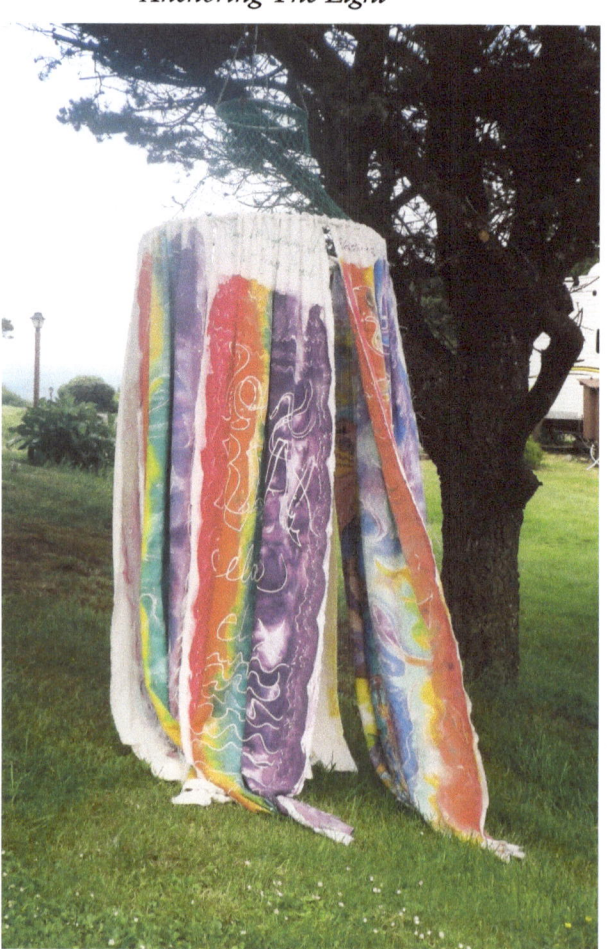

The Transformation Wheel®

©1993 **The Transformation Wheel®**
Trademarked practices, materials, and methods are available for one time reprint or use by permission of the artist. Trained facilitators may become licensed for full use.
For informtion, contact:
Billie Ruth Furuichi; *bilichki@gmail.com*

www.ingramcontent.com/pod-product-compliance
Lightning Source LLC
Chambersburg PA
CBHW050729180526
45159CB00003B/1174